ARTHUR SCHOPENHAUER was born in Danzig in 1788, where his family, of Dutch origin, owned one of the most respected trading houses. In 1793 the business moved to Hamburg, and in 1805 Arthur, who was expected to inherit it, was apprenticed as a clerk to another Hamburg house. He hated the work, so in 1807, two years after his father's suicide and the sale of the business, he enrolled at the grammar school at Gotha. In 1809 he entered Göttingen University to study medicine and science; the following year he took up philosophy. In 1811 he transferred to Berlin to write his doctoral thesis (1813). During the next four years he lived in Dresden and wrote *The World as Will and Idea* (1818), a complete exposition of his philosophy. Although the book failed to sell, Schopenhauer's belief in his own philosophy sustained him through twenty-five years of frustrated desire for fame. During his middle life, he travelled widely in Europe. In 1844 he brought out a greatly expanded edition of his book, which after his death became one of the most widely read of all philosophical works. His fame was established in 1851 with the publication of *Parerga and Paralipomena*, a large collection of essays, dialogues and aphorisms. From 1833 until his death from a heart attack in 1860 he lived in Frankfurt-am-Main.

R. J. HOLLINGDALE has translated works by, among others, Schopenhauer, Goethe, E. T. A. Hoffmann, Lichtenburg and Theodor Fontane, as well as eleven of Friedrich Nietzsche's books, many for the Penguin Classics. He has published two books about Nietzsche and is Honorary President of the British Nietzsche Society. He was for the Australian academic year 1991 Visiting Fellow at Trinity College, Melbourne.

ARTHUR SCHOPENHAUER

Essays and Aphorisms

*Selected and Translated with
an Introduction by*
R. J. HOLLINGDALE

PENGUIN BOOKS

PENGUIN BOOKS

Published by the Penguin Group
Penguin Books Ltd, 27 Wrights Lane, London W8 5TZ, England
Penguin Putnam Inc., 375 Hudson Street, New York, New York 10014, USA
Penguin Books Australia Ltd, Ringwood, Victoria, Australia
Penguin Books Canada Ltd, 10 Alcorn Avenue, Toronto, Ontario, Canada M4V 3B2
Penguin Books (NZ) Ltd, Private Bag 102902, NSMC, Auckland, New Zealand

Penguin Books Ltd, Registered Offices: Harmondsworth, Middlesex, England

This translation first published 1970
19 20 18

Translation and introduction copyright © R. J. Hollingdale, 1970
All rights reserved

Printed in England by Clays Ltd, St Ives plc
Set in Linotype Granjon

Except in the United States of America, this book is sold subject
to the condition that it shall not, by way of trade or otherwise, be lent,
re-sold, hired out, or otherwise circulated without the publisher's
prior consent in any form of binding or cover other than that in
which it is published and without a similar condition including this
condition being imposed on the subsequent purchaser

ARTHUR SCHOPENHAUER

Born in Danzig in February 1788
Died in Frankfurt-am-Main
in September 1860

CONTENTS

INTRODUCTION

Two Backgrounds

THIS volume contains a selection from Schopenhauer's last writings: the collection of essays, aphorisms and thoughts to which he gave the name *Parerga and Paralipomena*. Its object is to introduce the reader unfamiliar with them to the splendours and miseries of German metaphysics as reflected in the mirror of one very marked personality.

Schopenhauer is not difficult to understand provided one knows first something of the problems German metaphysical speculation was engaged in during his lifetime, and then something of his own background and experience. The combination – personal problems and subjective attitudes expressed in the language of metaphysics – is of the essence. Much of what in other nineteenth-century literatures went into novels, plays and poetry, in Germany went into philosophy, and this includes much of what was most original. There are no doubt other reasons for this, but one reason is certainly the overwhelming presence of Goethe. A dictum of Shaw's which seems to me obviously true is that the first great artist of any cultural epoch 'reaps the whole harvest and reduces those who come after to the rank of mere gleaners, or, worse than that, fools who go laboriously through all the motions of the reaper and binder in an empty field' (Preface to *Three Plays for Puritans*). The history of German literature in the nineteenth century is indeed only an exemplification of the truth of this dictum. The middle decades of the preceding century had been barren, but only in the way a field in spring is barren: the seed is down but it is not yet time for the harvest. In due course the harvest appeared, and Goethe reaped it all. In every category of 'literature' as usually understood he supplied the model instance: *Wilhelm Meister* was the model novel, the first part of *Faust* the model play, *Dichtung und Wahrheit* the model autobiography, the

9

Italienische Reise the model travel book; Eckermann's *Conversations with Goethe* – the 'best German book' in Nietzsche's opinion – is the German equivalent of Boswell's Johnson; the collected letters, which number over 13,000, is incomparably the greatest collection of its kind; and in poetry the comprehensiveness and size of his achievement threatened literally to exhaust the capacities of the German language, leaving nothing more to be done. One effect of all this was to drive original intellects out of the conventional literary categories into other fields, especially the field of philosophy, which Goethe had not harvested; and so it is that the world figures of German literature in the age after Goethe are not to be found among novelists or poets or dramatists, but among philosophers: Hegel, Schelling, Schopenhauer, Feuerbach, Marx, Nietzsche are the German peers of Tolstoy and Dostoyevsky, Balzac and Flaubert, Dickens and Mark Twain. The technical vocabulary they employ makes them harder to understand until that vocabulary is understood, and their employment of it often produces an atmosphere of impersonality and objectivity foreign to the world of the novel or the poem. A very intimate knowledge of Hegel, for example, is required to penetrate the 'scientific' outworks and gain the personality within: yet that personality determines the structure and nature of *The Phenomenology of the Spirit* just as surely as the personality of Dickens determines the structure and nature of *Our Mutual Friend*. But not every German metaphysician conceals himself so thoroughly as Hegel, who in any case suffered from genuine difficulty in expressing himself and who struggled consciously but in vain against an inadequate literary technique: the philosophy of Schelling is already more obviously the outcome of subjective attitudes in the individual who has framed it, and that of Schopenhauer is very clearly so. An individuality which under different circumstances might have expressed itself in fiction or poetry or autobiography here does so in the language of metaphysics and in terms of the perennial problems of metaphysics. The metaphysical problems dealt with are the common property of mankind, the individual subjectivity which deals with them produces a particular 'philosophy'. A necessary background for an easy and enjoyable reading of Schopenhauer's philosophical essays and aphorisms is, therefore, a knowledge of the fundamental problems he deals with – what he is writing about – and a knowledge of those elements in his personality and background which lead him to deal with these problems in just the way he does. Given this knowledge, Schopenhauer is as easy as Orwell (and Orwell is easy precisely because we know as soon as we start reading him what his problems are and against what background he is writing about them).[1]

Two Worlds

Let us begin with the metaphysical problem and let us try to make clear that it is a real problem and not something dreamed up by an idle or an over-refined mind. Let us go back to the beginning of philosophy and science, back to Thales, tradition-ally the first philosopher and scientist, because we shall find already in Thales the basic metaphysical problem Schopenhauer seeks to solve.

Thales is credited with the theory that everything is 'really' water. What does such an assertion mean? Why should it ever have occurred to anyone to say that everything was 'really' water? On the face of it, the theory is a statement about the physical world as conceived by the Greeks of the sixth century B.C.: it means that, of the four 'elements', three are forms of the

1. There is much in the present book which can be understood perfectly well without any knowledge of metaphysics or of Schopenhauer and which requires no explanation of any kind. The reader who feels like doing so could very well desert the Introduction at this point, go straight on to Schopenhauer and then see whether he comes up against any difficulty. If anyone quite unfamiliar with German philosophy and literature does this I believe he will find that, while dozens of pages are completely compre-hensible and many difficult only because of the author's employment of certain unfamiliar terms, the whole will nonetheless seem to rest on pre-suppositions and an attitude of mind which he is not entirely able to grasp, so that there will remain an unsatisfied feeling of somehow having failed to get the point of it all. The suggestions offered in the Introduction may then prove helpful to him.

fourth: earth is solidified water, air rarefied water, fire (aether, the hot sky of the eastern Mediterranean) rarefied air or twice-rarefied water. But merely in these physical terms the statement is inexplicable: for not only does it contradict the evidence of the five senses, it also seems to lack any necessity. Why should earth not be earth, air air and fire fire, as they seem to be? Now the inexplicability is in the idiom; the novelty is the language of physics, and in order to see what is meant we have to translate it back into its original language, that of metaphysics. Translated into the language of metaphysics, 'Everything is really water' reads: The world we perceive is characterized by great diversity, but this diversity is not fundamental; fundamentally the world is a unity. But notice that this unity is precisely what is *not* apparent; what is apparent is the reverse, the diversity of the world, and the object of the hypothesis is to assert the apparitional nature of this diversity. In its last significance, therefore, 'Everything is water' means: The world of diversity is an apparent world; in reality the world is one. Thus we find at the very beginning of philosophy the assertion that there exist two worlds, the 'real' and the 'apparent', that everything is 'really' something else and not what it 'appears' to be. If we are willing to call the language of physics employed by Thales the content of the thought, and the metaphysical basis of this language the form of the thought, we can say that the difference between scientific and pre-scientific thought is not so great a gulf as it is often supposed to be: the content of the thought is new, but its form remains the same, namely that there are two worlds, the one perceived, the other a mystery. Only if Thales had said 'Everything is really what it appears to be' would the form of the thought have changed.

This bifurcation of the world into the mundane world perceived and the transcendent, 'more real' world revealed by thinking is very probably an essential consequence of thinking as such, of the existence in the human head of a 'world of thought'. The most primitive men known to us already inhabit these two worlds. The fundamental idea is: I am *and* I think. From this idea there follows a second, derivative idea: there exists *another world*, the world I inhabit in my thinking. This 'other world' is *there*, exists, as an immediate consequence of the existence of thought in the human head: and as the race accumulates experience this world of thinking becomes massively enriched, especially by comparison with the almost static state of the world of perception, the outer, physical world. The earth consists once and for all of stones and plants and other animals; the sun rises and sets every day, summer and winter come round every year; the sea ebbs and flows, eternally the same; even men do not change very much, the new generation is much like the old: nature, in short, is the realm of the known, nature springs no surprises. But the world of thought and imagination is incredibly dynamic; it is continually expanding and changing and adding to itself new shapes and colours. The living occupy the world of nature, but the world of thought is also inhabited by the dead, and especially by the 'mighty dead', the founders and ancestors; indeed in this world they are no longer dead, they live on, they appear in dreams and waking dreams, they are immortal – and shall we too not be immortal, in that *other* world? The *supernatural* appears, with its gods and devils, heavens and hells, in that second world of thought and imagination. In memory the *past*, that which has vanished from the perceived world, continues to exist – *where* does it exist? In that other world which we perceive only in thought. The ties and limitations of the physical world disappear in that other world, we are free of them, we can do anything; but at the same time it is only there that we encounter actual *terror*, the terror which hovers about the abode of the god and which stalks the sleeper when, dead to the physical world, he enters that other world wholly and wanders about in it. Is it any wonder, then, that this second world, the world of thought, comes to be *much more real* than the physical world, that men should come to regard it as *alone real*, as 'the real world'? And once this step has been taken, is it not likely that the physical world will be progressively devalued for the benefit of the 'real' world, that all the qualities in it which men find useful or interesting or dreadful will be transferred one by one to the 'real' world as to their true home, so that at last the physical world is denuded of all value and claim to veneration and becomes a mere illusion, an appearance, a veil masking that other, 'real' world?

Before philosophy, before rational thinking at all, it is there: the world as appearance and the world as reality. Mythology and primitive religion speak directly of this transference of value; philosophy and sophisticated religion do so more covertly. By the sixth century B.C. the idea of two worlds is so firmly a part of human consciousness that even Kung Fu-tse, the very model of the secular prophet, assumes it, and the Buddha in India, Zarathustra in Persia and Isaiah in Palestine preach it constantly. In Ionia the content of the idea undergoes a re-markable change, but the form remains the same: the *physio-logoi,* as Aristotle names them, the 'investigators of nature', begin to speak the language of science and philosophy, but still they answer the old metaphysical question 'Is the world what it appears to be?' in the negative. 'Reality' is still something that lurks behind the scenes. Thales says that reality is water. Hera-clitus says it is 'an ever-living fire' and the 'real world' the battleground for an eternal conflict and for ceaseless change: change is 'real'; unity and permanence are 'appearance'. Accord-ing to Parmenides change is logically impossible, an illusion: 'reality' is motionless, unchanging being. Anaxagoras taught that all four 'elements' are present in everything, so that water also contains earth, air and fire, though in small quantity com-pared with the quantity of water: water appears to be water; in reality it is a compound of earth, air, water and fire. Demo-critus propounded the atomic theory, or the doctrine that solidity is appearance. Only this tradition – the tradition that the seeming is not the real – can, with an ingredient from the old-fashioned mysticism of Pythagoras and Empedocles, account for the philosophy of Plato, in whose doctrine of supra-sensible Forms the primitive notion of a real and an apparent world receives its most coherent expression. Everyone knows Plato's parable of the men sitting in a dark cave with their backs to the light watching the play of their shadows: the shadows are the 'world', the light comes from the 'real world'. In Plato the physical universe has been devalued to a shadow-play on the wall.

Platonism is the conceptual basis of Christianity. The actual bridge is the so-called Neo-Platonism of Plotinus, in which the crumbling Roman Empire is contrasted with the supernal realm of beauty and order which alone is asserted to be real. Plotinus's real world is almost the Christian heaven, his Roman Empire almost the Christian kingdom of this world: all that is lacking is a god. With the victory of Christianity all positive value is transferred to the Beyond. Moreover: 'Now we see through a glass, darkly; but then face to face: now I know in part; but then shall I know even as also I am known' – in other words, *this* world is a veil obscuring the light of reality. From Paul to Augustine the history of Christianity is the history of a progressively widening gap between the two worlds, until in its final form Christianity *means* duality: the duality of Church and State, Pope and Emperor, this world and the next, the City of God and the Earthly City, God and his creation, the individual souls of men and the Holy Spirit 'in whom we are all one' – all ultimately forms of that primeval duality of the world in the eyes and the world in the mind.

Modern philosophy begins by restoring to this primeval duality its simplest form of expression: Descartes' solution to the riddle of the universe is that there are two and only two existants in the world of created things: thinking substance or soul and extended substance or matter. These are the two worlds of man undisguised. Descartes is very sober – a great virtue after the metaphysical debauch of the Middle Ages. He does not even suggest that the thinking substance is 'more real' than the extended substance: appearance and reality is not a problem for him, or rather it is a problem he refuses to get involved in. How are the thinking and the extended substances, soul and matter, united in man? Descartes says he does not know and turns to other things. But 'I don't know' is water, and mankind wants something stronger: 'I don't know' won't do. Spinoza, the subtlest of all distillers of metaphysics, provides what is needed: soul and matter, says Spinoza, are not substances;

there is only one substance, God; God is infinite and has an infinite number of modes of being; of these we know two, thought and extension; soul and matter are therefore modes of one underlying substance. Everything is 'really' God.

The relationship between Descartes and Spinoza is repeated in the relationship between Locke and Berkeley, and it is through this line that the great problem ultimately reaches the ears of Schopenhauer. Locke starts from the material world, which to him is what is given and self-evident. In addition to the material world there is an immaterial world which acts on the sense organs and, through these, produces 'ideas' in the human brain: these are of two kinds, 'ideas of sensation' – the physical world as perceived – and 'ideas of reflexion' – the operation of the mind upon the ideas of sensation and in fact the 'world of thought'. Locke freely admits he does not know how the stimulation of sense organs produces ideas, but what he does claim to know is that knowledge of the material world consists in the 'ideas' of it we have in our minds. Like Descartes, Locke lacks mystery: instead of mystification there is confession of ignorance. Enter upon the scene Bishop Berkeley, his soul full of distaste for the 'materialism' of Locke. If, says Berkeley, our knowledge of the material world consists in the ideas of it we have in our heads, what reason is there for supposing that anything other than the ideas exists? Locke, like Descartes, concludes that the world is what it seems to be: a material thing and a mental thing, a collection of pieces of material and a collection of mental ideas. But Locke goes on to say that all the mind can know is the mental ideas and thus, says Berkeley, deprives us of any ground for supposing that the pieces of material exist. Suppose the material world did *not* exist: would anything about our perception of the world be changed? If all we know is the mental ideas nothing would be changed. The material world is an unnecessary and undemonstrable hypothesis: so away with it. Berkeley abolishes matter and declares the world to be a creation of mind. Everything is 'really' mind.

Now this conclusion is to the commonsense mind fantastic. Johnson kicking a stone and declaring 'I thus refute him!' is likely to represent the normal reaction to it. But I would ask the reader to observe, firstly that it is no more 'fantastic' than any other hypothesis which asserts the superior reality of some world other than the physical, and secondly that it does actually follow from the conclusions of Locke, which nobody in the eighteenth century regarded as anything but the plainest sense. The reason Berkeley's conclusion seems so very odd is that it is insufficiently radical: it assumes too much of what is in fact old-style commonsense, so that the arguments Berkeley offers in support of it are merely ingenious rather than convincing. Locke points not towards the simple substitution of one kind of knowledge for another, but towards a radical critique of knowledge itself, a thorough-going analysis and assessment of what it is we really know. This critique is undertaken by David Hume. Hume asserts that our mind consists of 'impressions' and 'ideas'. Impressions are what Locke had called 'ideas of sensation', our perception of the physical world; ideas are images of impressions, formed in thinking and reasoning: *ergo* we can have no idea of anything of which we have received no impression. What has not been perceived cannot be known. You think you know fire causes heat, says Hume, but you do not know that, because causation is not something perceived. You can perceive that A is bigger than B or on top of B or always accompanied by B, but you cannot perceive that it causes B. 'Causation' is the expectation that what has always been conjoined in the past will always be conjoined in the future: but you cannot know that the future resembles the past because what does not yet exist cannot be perceived: you *suppose* it will, but that is a matter of habit. The consequence is that real knowledge of the world is fragmentary; that we have connected knowledge of it is an illusion born of habit and laziness.

Kant read Hume and it changed his life. He wanted to contradict him but couldn't: he found him irrefutable. And yet he *must* somehow have gone wrong, since it was impossible permanently to acquiesce in the notion that the reasoning powers of mankind were illusory. When he finally detected *how* Hume had gone wrong his solution was the foundation of 'German metaphysics' in the modern sense and provided the immediate background to the metaphysics of Schopenhauer. Kant's undertaking is a new description of the human mind. It falls, he says, into two parts: the part which perceives and the part which thinks (*vide* Locke's 'ideas of sensation' and 'ideas of reflexion' and Hume's 'impressions' and 'ideas'). The perceiving part of the mind receives the impressions conveyed by the senses, and Kant calls these impressions 'particulars'; the thinking part is the organ of the understanding and the objects of the understanding. he calls 'concepts'. The application of concepts to particulars constitutes 'synthetic judgements'. What is a synthetic judgement? 'Judgement' is Kant's term for 'proposition', and he first classifies judgements as being either analytic or synthetic. An analytic judgement is one whose predicate is contained in its subject, so that its denial is a self-contradiction. (Example: all mothers are female – analytic because 'mother' means 'a female parent'.) A synthetic judgement is one whose predicate is not contained in its subject, so that its denial is not a self-contradiction: thus all judgements (propositions) which, in ordinary terms, 'say something' are synthetic. Now synthetic judgements are also of two kinds: *a posteriori* and *a priori*. A synthetic *a posteriori* judgement is one whose truth or falsity can be determined by experience. (Example: cake is fattening.) A synthetic *a priori* judgement is one which is independent of experience. (Example: every event has a cause – synthetic because its predicate is not contained in its subject, *a priori* because it is independent of experience, *vide* Hume.) And Kant maintains that scientific, mathematical and moral judgements are all synthetic *a priori*.

What he has done up to this point is to define the type of proposition asserted by Hume to be impossible. We cannot say 'A causes B', Hume had declared, because we cannot know it. Kant's retort is that we *do* say 'A causes B' and a great many more things of the same kind: and his concern is to discover *how* it comes about that we do so. How are synthetic *a priori* judgements *possible*? is the question he asks. His answer is as follows: The *concepts* – the objects of the understanding – are of three types: *a posteriori* (abstracted from sense perception and applied to it), *a priori* (applicable to sense perception but not abstracted from it), and a third type called Ideas, which are concepts neither abstracted from sense perception nor applicable to it. The *a priori* concepts of science and other forms of knowledge he calls 'categories'. Consider 'Every event has a cause': this synthetic *a priori* judgement is not derived from sense perception, since causation cannot be perceived, but it is applied to the objects of sense perception: the concept of causation is thus an *a priori* concept, and causation is thus a category. There are twelve categories in all. Synthetic *a priori* judgements consist in applying the categories to the perceptions of sense in time and space. Sense perception in time and space he calls the perceptual manifold: the categories are not derived from the manifold but *imposed upon* it, and this – the imposition of the categories upon the perceptual manifold – constitutes 'thinking'. It will now follow that an 'object' is that which is capable of conforming to the categories; if it cannot do so, it cannot exist for a human observer. The answer to the question 'How are synthetic *a priori* judgements possible?' is that they are the structure imposed *by* the mind *upon* the world.

But see what follows then: if the mind imposes a certain structure upon the world in order to apprehend it, this presupposes that the world upon which this structure is imposed exists independently of it, that there must exist something upon which to impose it: and this something Kant calls the 'thing in itself' – the object of perception as it 'really' is, before and independently of the imposition of the categories of reason. The object as perceived under the forms of the categories he calls 'phenomenon' or 'appearance'. The ultimate conclusion is that there are two worlds: the 'real' world (the thing in itself) and the 'apparent' world (the world of phenomena).

I have recited all this Kantian jargon, and thus risked boring the reader unfamiliar with it, partly because Kant's ideas are essentially incommunicable without it and it is thus a paradigm of that technical vocabulary which has always hindered appreciation of German philosophy and concealed the personalities of German philosophers, but partly also to try to bring home the seeming inevitability with which, at the stage of thought we are concerned with, mankind must divide the world in which it lives into two worlds, the one immediate and visible but of an inferior degree of reality, the other hidden, requiring discovery, but *more real*. In its popular acceptance Kant's philosophy has always meant above all a rigorously scientific demonstration that appearance is not reality.

Now if he is able to remember all that has gone before, I believe the reader will not experience any sense of shock when introduced to a philosophy which begins with 'The world is my idea' and ends by asserting that the physical universe, with its stars and galaxies and Milky Ways, is 'nothing', but that the philosophy of Schopenhauer will, as metaphysics, seem to him no more than a natural continuation of the fundamental drift of the human mind.

The World as Will and Idea

Schopenhauer thought that he alone had understood Kant correctly, and he dismissed Kant's other successors, especially Hegel, as charlatans. His first act is to interpret Kant in a Berkeleian sense: he equates Kant's phenomena with Berkeley's ideas in the mind and says with Berkeley that the world as it is perceived is a creation of the intellect which perceives it. This he takes to have been proved by Kant, but in any case self-evidently obvious; so that he is able to open the book in which he expounds his philosophy, *The World as Will and Idea*, with the flat assertion 'The world is my idea'. This takes care of 'idea': but what about 'my'? what of the 'I' which has the idea? Schopenhauer thinks the existence of this 'I' an absolute necessity, in the same way as the existence of an 'apparent' world makes necessary the existence of a 'real' world: and in fact this 'I' *is* the real world, the substratum of the world of phenomena. Now it will be clear that if we have knowledge of ourselves, of this 'I', it will be a different kind of knowledge from that which we have of anything else. All other kinds of knowledge amount to establishing relations between ideas, but knowledge of oneself would be knowledge of immediate reality. And this is what Schopenhauer maintains knowledge of oneself actually is. We know ourselves objectively, in the same way as we know all other phenomena, as an object extended in space and time: we know ourselves as body. But we also know ourselves subjectively, we have an inner consciousness of our own existence, and we possess feelings and desires. This inner world Schopenhauer calls 'will': we know ourselves as will. And thus there follows the 'single thought' which, properly understood, Schopenhauer says constitutes the whole of his philosophy: 'My body and my will are one'. My body is the phenomenal form of my will, my will is the noumenal form of my body: my body is 'appearance', my will 'thing in itself'.

Now if this is true of *my* body, it is true of every other body, consequently of every other phenomenon. I am aware of myself as will and idea, a block of stone is not aware at all: but that is the only difference between us in regard to the point under discussion: the block of stone is also noumenon and phenomenon, thing in itself and appearance, will and idea: its body and its will are one, only its will has not attained to consciousness. Furthermore, since Kant had proved that space and time, the spatial and temporal fragmentation of the world, belonged as forms of perception only to the plane of phenomena, the noumenal plane, the 'real world' of the thing in itself, must be one and indivisible: consequently the will in the stone and the will in me is the same will. Thus the world is a duality: the 'world as idea' is the outer, physical world, the realm of time, space and causation, 'appearance', Kant's phenomenal world; the 'world as will' is the inner, subjective world, not subject to the forms of space and time, a unity, 'reality', Kant's noumenal world or thing in itself.

This, I think, is all it is necessary to say about the metaphysical basis of Schopenhauer's philosophy: to say more would be to anticipate what he himself says in the essays and aphorisms which follow. But that the world is a duality of will and idea is the minimum the reader has to bear in mind, because Schopenhauer assumes it as a given fact and unless the reader does so too (for the purpose of reading him) he will often fail to see what Schopenhauer is driving at.

The Pessimistic Outlook

So much, then, for the metaphysical background to Schopenhauer's writings: 'the world as will and idea' is not an eccentricity but simply a new content for an old form. Now for the real novelty, the decisive element deriving from the philosopher's personality. For a while metaphysics seems to be Schopenhauer's whole or main concern: it comes as a surprise therefore to discover that the elaborate metaphysical structure has been brought into existence not for its own sake but for the sake of something else, something much more personal than an abstract account of the nature of reality. We learn that this extraordinary man has created a new metaphysic and constructed a new model of the universe simply in order to understand and justify his own pessimistic disposition. There have been great pessimists before: we have our own great pessimist, whose last word to us was that we are such stuff as dreams are made on: but there has been none who tried with so great a show of learning to demonstrate that the pessimistic outlook is *justified*, that life itself really is bad. It is to *this* end that Schopenhauer's metaphysic of will and idea exists: the hinge of his philosophy is the ethical assertion that will is evil and must be 'denied'.

Every individual is embodied will, and the nature of will is to strive to live – will is 'will to live'. This means that fundamentally every individual is an ego whose interest in staying alive overrides every other, including of course the life-interest of every other individual. The outcome is universal conflict. The suffering engendered by this conflict is the normal and inescapable condition of life, and happiness means merely the diminution of suffering, i.e. happiness is negative. The way out of this circle of suffering lies in denial of the will, refusal to enter the contest: the power to do so is provided by the conscious intellect, which is capable of understanding the nature of the will and its effects and thus of striving to set them aside. Ultimately the only real good is extinction: the realization that the perceived universe – the 'world as idea' – is as nothing, the conscious acceptance of the need for annihilation as the only true cure for the sickness of life, and finally the acceptance of annihilation itself.

This very brief outline of Schopenhauer's ethics is likely to raise more questions than it answers: but, again, to explain in greater detail would be to anticipate the body of the book. It is enough here to grasp that the idealist metaphysics exists in order to serve the pessimistic outlook.

Now just as it was, in my opinion, necessary to show that Schopenhauer's metaphysic is not an oddity or aberration, so in order to try to discover the origin and meaning of his pessimistic ethic we ought now to examine his life, since the ethic is very clearly the subjective element in his philosophy, as well as being the decisive element. What kind of life was it that produced, that made necessary, so pessimistic a response in him who suffered it?

An Immovable Mind

Let us go straightaway to the heart of the man, to his most pronounced and enduring characteristic. Here, with all possible brevity, are five details from his biography which, I believe, all exhibit the same tendency, are all obviously the acts of the same man.

1. Schopenhauer's philosophy is stated, complete in all its details, in *The World as Will and Idea*. The book was published at the end of 1818 but its fundamental ideas had been in Schopenhauer's head for about four years and can be said to have been fully formed by 1816 at the latest. In 1816 Schopenhauer was 28. Now everything he subsequently wrote was elaboration or confirmation of or comment on the philosophy of *The World as Will and Idea*: he adds nothing and subtracts nothing. The mind of the man of 70 is wholly occupied with the ideas of the man of 28: he has acquired more knowledge but nothing he

has subsequently learned has induced him to change his mind in any particular.

2. In May 1819 Schopenhauer learned that the Danzig business house in which his mother and sister had most of their money invested had gone bankrupt. He himself also had a small amount invested. The company offered to pay 30 per cent; when Schopenhauer was told his mother and sister were going to accept this offer he wrote demanding 70 per cent of what was owed to *him*, and that if this should not be forthcoming instantly he would demand 100 per cent. He then fought a two-year legal battle to get his money back: his claim amounted to about one-fiftieth of the total liabilities of the bankrupt house, but while every other creditor finally settled for 30 per cent he persisted in refusing to do so and at length received back the full amount due to him, plus the accumulated interest.

3. Schopenhauer decided to become a university lecturer in philosophy. He opened his course at Berlin in the summer of 1820 and chose as his lecture time the precise hours at which Hegel, who was also at Berlin, delivered his principal course. Schopenhauer, an unknown man, lectured to an empty room and continued to do so until it was borne in upon him that he would have either to change his hours or abandon his course: he abandoned his course and with it his career as a university lecturer.

4. One day in August 1821, still in Berlin, Schopenhauer was involved in an altercation at his lodgings with a sempstress, one Caroline Luise Marguet, aged 47, which ended with his throwing her down the stairs. He alleged she was making too much noise; she maintained she was only talking to a friend on the landing and sued him for injuries which, she claimed, made it impossible for her to carry on her profession. Schopenhauer resisted the claim and litigation dragged on for nearly five years; at one moment, while he was visiting Italy, all his goods and property in Berlin were placed under distraint until he should return to attend court. In March 1826 he was sentenced to pay Mlle Marguet 60 talers (about £9) a year for the rest of her life.

She lived until 1852: when Schopenhauer received a copy of her death certificate he wrote across it: *Obit anus, abit onus* (the old woman dies, the debt departs).

5. From the age of 45 until his death 27 years later Schopenhauer lived in Frankfurt-am-Main. He lived alone, in 'rooms', and every day for 27 years he followed an identical routine. He rose every morning at seven and had a bath but no breakfast: he drank a cup of strong coffee before sitting down at his desk and writing until noon. At noon he ceased work for the day and spent half-an-hour practising the flute, on which he became quite a skilled performer. Then he went out for lunch at the Englischer Hof. After lunch he returned home and read until four, when he left for his daily walk: he walked for two hours no matter what the weather. At six o'clock he visited the reading room of the library and read *The Times*. In the evening he attended the theatre or a concert, after which he had dinner at a hotel or restaurant. He got back home between nine and ten and went early to bed. He was willing to deviate from this routine in order to receive visitors: but with this exception he carried it through for 27 years.

The temperamental quality which these details all exemplify goes by different names depending on the nature of the circumstances under which it is manifested. In regard to 1 it might be called constancy or fixity, in regard to 2 perseverance or doggedness, in regard to 3 obstinacy or self-will, in regard to 4 pigheadedness or intractability, in regard to 5 inertia or immovability. If we try for a non-emotive description we might call it the inability to abandon or modify an attitude of mind once adopted. Consider the daily two-hour walk. Among Schopenhauer's disciples of the late nineteenth century this walk was a celebrated fact of his biography, and it was so because of its regularity. There was speculation as to why he insisted on going out and staying out for two hours no matter what the weather. It suggests health fanaticism, but there is no other evidence that Schopenhauer was a health fanatic or a crank. In my view the reason was simply obstinacy: he *would* go out and nothing would stop him. It is a minor manifestation of that rooted immovability of mind. (Schopenhauer's definition of obstinacy will be found on page 170. I think that by the time the reader comes to it he will find it less a definition of obstinacy than a splendid instance of it.)

My purpose in flogging this point is to try to make it seem at any rate possible that, if a pessimistic attitude towards life had grown up in Schopenhauer's mind as a result of his early experience of it, that attitude would persist unchanged throughout his adult years and down to his death; so that the cause of his pessimistic disposition could plausibly be sought in youthful experiences which, while in themselves not at all uncommon, might make on him an uncommonly lasting impression. What would then be singular about Schopenhauer would not be his pessimism itself but only the fact that it endured long enough for him to bring to its exposition and analysis the power of a very gifted *adult* intelligence. For that disillusionment with life which Schopenhauer expounds and tries to account for in almost all his writings was the consequence not of any unique or very uncommon occurrence but of experiences which tens of thousands and perhaps millions of other young men have undergone in our epoch, experiences which have brought the taste of ashes to their mouth and whose effects they have overcome or even forgotten simply because they lacked Schopenhauer's immovability of mind.

Early Life

The family background of almost all German philosophers has been scholarly or clerical: their fathers have been teachers or clergymen. Schopenhauer's father was a trader and his family background was mercantile. In origin the Schopenhauers were Dutch, and Heinrich Floris Schopenhauer (1747–1805) is a recognizable Dutch type: a businessman with a taste for culture and stylish living. At the end of the seventeenth century or the beginning of the eighteenth the family settled in the great mercantile port and free city of Danzig on the Baltic, and Heinrich Floris, together with his brother Johann Friedrich, built up the house of Schopenhauer into one of the most stable and reputable in the city. He is described as having a 'square, muscular frame, broad face with wide mouth and prominent underjaw' – which might be a description of his son in his later years. When Prussia annexed Danzig in March 1793 as part of the second partition of Poland, the house of Schopenhauer moved out of a city no longer 'free' and transferred to Hamburg, where H. F. Schopenhauer conducted business for 12 years without ever becoming naturalized. The hysteria behind the stiff façade of the bourgeois merchant and necessitating it lay close to the surface in Heinrich Floris, and in his last years he developed signs of mental unbalance. In April 1805 he was found lying dead in a canal, apparently having fallen from a granary abutting on to it: his associates and family were in little doubt that he had committed suicide.

This was Arthur Schopenhauer's father. His mother was a very different type of human being. Johanna Henrietta, born Trosiener (1766–1838), was also a Danziger and the daughter of a merchant, but her tastes were totally at variance with those of her world. She had a very easy-going disposition and enjoyed party-going and party-giving; she was also 'artistic' in the silly sense and a bit of a culture snob; but on the whole a much more pleasing personality than Heinrich Floris. His death was a release: she wound up the house of Schopenhauer and, together with her daughter Adele (1796–1849), Arthur's only sister, she went to live in Weimar, the capital of German classical literature, where in due course she embarked on a literary career herself and ran a salon at which Goethe and other notables appeared from time to time. She was the author of several novels and achieved a moderate fame of which Arthur, when he too had become an author, was envious. (It was one of the many subjects they quarrelled about. An exchange which has been preserved – Arthur: My book will be available when all your books are completely forgotten. Johanna: Yes, the whole edition will be available.)

When Arthur was born, in Danzig on 22 February 1788, it was to this not very well matched couple and as inheritor of their barely compatible qualities. But his earliest years were very happy: there was always plenty of money and although cared for almost exclusively by his mother, who lived on the Schopenhauer farm at the eastern limit of Danzig territory while his father stayed most of the week in the city itself, he was decidedly his father's son. Heinrich Floris intended, of course, that he should inherit the house of Schopenhauer and he was brought up with that destiny in view. His schooling was sporadic and in 1797, aged nine, he was taken off to Paris and then Le Havre, where he stayed for two years with a French family. In 1799 he came back, not to Danzig but to Hamburg, and for three years attended a private school 'for the sons of the wealthier classes'. During these years the maternal component of his make-up began to become active and he developed a strong inclination towards literature which at length dominated him and led him to declare his intention of following a literary career when he grew up. It is clear that neither he nor his father had any precise notion of what this meant, but his father did know that at any rate it did not sound compatible with running the house of Schopenhauer as it ought to be run. He therefore offered the boy an alternative: either he could persist in wanting a 'literary career', in which case he would have to begin regular studies in Hamburg of literature, Latin and other dull subjects; or he could agree to settle down to a mercantile career, in which case he could leave immediately on a long tour of France and England so as to see something of the world first. Arthur was 15 and he chose the latter alternative. Presumably his father knew he would. They all left for a trip that was to last two years (1803-5), and when they returned to Hamburg in January 1805 Arthur was put into the office of a merchant named Jenisch, as a clerk.

This is now the crucial epoch of his life. In April his father dies: the death leaves him feeling more rather than less bound to fulfil his promise to become a merchant. But the house of Schopenhauer is sold up, his mother and sister leave for Weimar, and he is left in the office of Jenisch. And now despair begins to enter his soul. He hates the work of a clerk, and has now come to hate the whole mercantile world; at the same time his very modest education has fitted him for little else. When he is 21 he will get his share of the paternal fortune, assuming his mother has not spent it by then – but as yet he is only 17, and at 17 four years are an unimaginable eternity. In short, Jenisch's office becomes Schopenhauer's blacking factory – with this difference, that Dickens's experience was that of a little boy unable to analyse his situation and was one now fortunately rare, while Schopenhauer's is so ordinary as to be called perhaps the common lot of middle-class youth. The capitalist world, and in particular the heart of it, the world of buying and selling, offers almost nothing a young man wants: the instincts of youth are at variance with the demands of business, and especially with those of clerking. What young man is by nature diligent, sober and regular in his habits? Respectful to 'superiors' and humble before wealth? Sincerely able to devote himself to what he finds boring? One in ten thousand, perhaps. But for the great majority a 'job' is, depending on temperament, a torment or a tedious irrelevance which has to be endured day after day in order that, during one's so-called 'free time', one will be allowed to get on with living. The situation is the most commonplace in the world. I believe it is the cause of that settled cynicism with which nine out of ten regard the 'social order': they know that, short of a total revolution in the conduct of human affairs, any conceivable social order will for the great majority mean the boredom of routine, the damming up of their natural energies and the frustration of their natural desires. This familiar feeling was what now overcame Schopenhauer: the feeling which appears when life, hitherto apparently capable of granting anything, is suddenly revealed as a deception, when the colour is drained from it and the whole future seems a single grey. The essence is in the question: *Is this all?* Is *this* life? The intensity with which the question is asked must of course vary: but when we consider that Schopenhauer was in fact a man of genius, we shall not be surprised to discover that in him its intensity was very great. He himself tells us that, when in the spring of 1807 his mother wrote to him from Weimar that now two years had elapsed he could if he wished regard his promise to his late father as fulfilled and change his mode of life, he 'burst into tears of joy' and left Jenisch's office at once. And my contention is that the attitude towards life produced by these two years and more of office misery became, as did everything he felt, a permanent and irremovable part of his make-up: became, in fact, his permanent attitude towards life. What he as yet lacks is a mode of expressing it, but as soon as he is introduced to a suitable mode he seizes it instantly and employs it to the limit of its capacity.

Self-discovery

He is now 19, and only now does he embark on any kind of higher education. In June 1807 he goes to the grammar school at Gotha and subsequently to Weimar. He soon manages to find the amount of money his mother spends extravagant because, as he sees it, it has all been earned by his father; he also resents the evident fact that the 'widow' has certainly not resigned herself to lovelessness. He quarrels with her and from then on they are never on a friendly footing.

In February 1809, at 21, he receives his share of the patrimony and is now well off and his own master. His first act is to enter himself at Göttingen University, to which he goes in October to study medicine and science. After a year he turns to philosophy, and at once knows he has found himself. He is already 22, but by the time he is 28 he has formulated in every detail the philosophy of 'will and idea' which is the complete expression of his personality and whose vehicle, *The World as Will and Idea*, is half a century later to become the Koran of a large and very variously composed cult.

His teacher, G. E. Schulze, advised him to confine his reading to Plato and Kant: this he did, almost literally. Plato and Kant (with one other ingredient to be mentioned later) provided him with all the conceptual machinery he needed to formulate his own ideas in philosophical language. In 1811 he transferred to the University of Berlin, then in only the second year of its

existence, and heard Fichte lecture, though without either pleasure or profit: his ideas were already fixed, and in any case
Fichte was at this time coming forward as the great champion
of German nationhood, a cause to which Schopenhauer was
totally indifferent. In 1813 the German states rose against
Napoleon and after the battle of Lützen (2 May), when Berlin
appeared to be in danger, he left that city for Dresden and subsequently Rudolstadt, where he wrote his doctoral thesis,
originally meant for Berlin, now offered to Jena. He received
his diploma on 2 October, and in November returned to Weimar.
He tried to resume relations with his mother but they quarrelled
afresh and when he left the town in May 1814 he never saw her
again. From 1814 to 1818 he lived in Dresden, and there he
wrote *The World as Will and Idea*. To Plato and Kant he had
now added the reading of a curiosity of early nineteenth-century
literature: the Upanishads in Anquetil Duperron's Latin translation of a Persian version of the Sanskrit original, published in
1801 and 1802. This introduced him to Indian metaphysics,
and again he required nothing more (or very little: while in
Dresden he met the orientalist Friedrich Majer, whose *Brahma,
or The Religion of the Hindus* appeared in 1819, and no doubt
learned something from him). The Upanishads supplied the
ultimate confirmation of his pessimistic ethic and made it possible for him to employ the metaphysic of Kant in a sense remote
from that in which Kant himself had employed it. Of *The
World as Will and Idea* its author himself had the highest
opinion. 'Subject to the limitation of human knowledge,' he
wrote, 'my philosophy is the real solution of the enigma of the
world. In this sense it may be called a revelation. It is inspired
by the spirit of truth: in the fourth book there are even some
paragraphs which may be considered to be dictated by the Holy
Ghost.' Such was his self-confidence, and he certainly needed
some during the coming decades: the book, when it appeared at
the end of 1818, was an utter failure: nobody bought it, nobody
read it, nobody reviewed it. But until it began to be noticed in
the 1850s, Schopenhauer survived virtually on his confidence
that it would one day find its public and that one day he would

be famous: for his desire for fame amounted almost to a mania
– in later years, when he had acquired 'disciples', he employed
them in combing the newspapers and periodicals of Europe for
references to himself and his work. Moreover, in *The World as
Will and Idea* he had expressed himself so completely that he
published nothing further for 18 years.

Later Life

In the summer of 1831 cholera attacked Berlin. Among those
who died was Hegel, among those who fled Schopenhauer. He
went to Frankfurt-am-Main, in the following summer transferred to Mannheim but returned to Frankfurt at the beginning
of June 1833. He lived in Frankfurt in the manner described
until his death from a heart attack on 21 September 1860. Since
the publication of *The World as Will and Idea* his 'work' had
consisted chiefly of seeking out confirmations of the thesis there
expounded. In 1836 he published *On the Will in Nature*, designed to show that scientific knowledge corroborated his metaphysics. In 1838 the Scientific Society of Drontheim, Norway,
offered a prize for an essay on 'whether free will could be proved
from the evidence of consciousness'. Schopenhauer's essay, ready
by February 1839, won the prize, and he subsequently entered a further essay for a prize offered by the Royal Danish
Academy of the Sciences for a discussion of the source or
foundation of morality: in this case, however, his essay, the
only one submitted, was rejected. He published them both in
1841 under the title *The Two Fundamental Problems of Ethics*.
All three works are no more than footnotes to *The World as
Will and Idea*.

But he had also by this time begun writing what was finally
to amount to a very large quantity of essays, aphorisms and
reflexions, some bearing directly on his philosophy, others only
obliquely. Despite its continuing lack of success, he persuaded
its publisher, Brockhaus of Leipzig, to bring out a second
edition of *The World as Will and Idea*: the large amount of
additional material incorporated was in the nature of expansion

of and comment on the existing book. After the appearance of this new edition he began to attract some little attention, but it was still not for another seven years that he published his second, and last, major book, *Parerga and Paralipomena*, which appeared in 1851. It was this very large but loosely assembled collection which first gained him wide popularity. It was declined by three publishers and finally brought out by Hayn of Berlin, at the prompting of Julius Frauenstädt, his first genuine follower: the only payment he received was ten free copies. During the 1850s he was able to savour something of the fame he desired; but nothing short of universal acclaim could have satisfied him, and death denied him anything he could have considered a triumph: it was not until the succeeding decades that his philosophy made its real mark.

The older Schopenhauer, who is the author of the present book, is much the same man who wept tears of joy at being freed from Jenisch's office. His mental life is devoted to reflexion: the outer world is chiefly material for reflexion. This is already true of the notes he made during his English tour of 1803–5, and is true of those he made during a tour of Italy in 1818: they consist almost always of the reflexions to which impressions give rise, hardly ever of the impressions themselves. He told the ageing Wieland when he met him in Weimar: 'Life is a *missliche Sache* – a disagreeable thing –: I have determined to spend it in reflecting on it.' This was not idle chatter: it describes what he actually did. There are gaping lacunae in his biography, especially in the 1820s, during which nothing worthy of note happened to him at all: objectively he was merely idling his years away, actually his love of reflecting and brooding was during these periods absorbing all his time.

Or almost all: like many very intellectual men he had a strongly sensual side to his nature, and his sexual interest was very strong. He had many erotic affairs, none of them lasting: indeed, 'affairs' is probably the wrong word, since it implies attachments of longer duration than most of Schopenhauer's – in his own day his sexual activity would have been called philandering when it involved women of his own class, whoring when it involved those of a lower class. In politics he was a believer in monarchy and rule from above, but in sex he was a perfect democrat: he considered all women equal. The position of sexuality in his philosophy is a direct reflexion of his personal situation. His famous misogyny is really his reaction to the way his mother was able to find a new and more satisfying life after his father's death – another instance of the retention of an attitude adopted in early life: without overdriving the comparison one could say that his was the reaction of Hamlet. His 'affairs' might then be seen as a meting-out of punishment to the female sex. On the other hand, the strength of his sexual drive was certainly considerable in itself, and when he condemns it as the actual centre and intensest point of the 'will to live' he speaks from experience: his fundamental feeling towards it was undoubtedly that he was its victim, that he was 'in thrall' to it. In his best recorded moments Schopenhauer understands more vividly than anyone the suffering involved in life and the need felt by all created things for love and sympathy: at these moments he knew and hated the coldness and egoism of his own sensuality.

Grounds of His Success

We have looked, as briefly as possible, at the source of Schopenhauer's metaphysics and then at that of his pessimism. It remains to indicate the source of his success. To begin with, the pessimism itself struck a responsive chord. Many found it a great relief to cast off for once the *obbligato* optimism of our culture and to face the possibility that things may not be all for the best. That was one element. Another was his freedom from conventional religious sentiment. All previous German philosophers had set out from Christianity and had endeavoured in some way to justify its fundamental assumptions: Schopenhauer reinterpreted Christianity in a pessimistic sense, and then assimilated it to the religions of the East, in order to draw it into the orbit of his own philosophy: but this philosophy itself was atheist. The 'will' is not God: there *is* no God in Schopenhauer's world of will and idea. Not to have to reconcile the evil of the world with the existence of God – that was another great relief.

A third reason for Schopenhauer's ultimate success was his thesis that will is primary, intellect secondary. It cannot be truly said that he himself is 'anti-rationalist'; I do not see how any reader of the following pieces could consider him anything but a close reasoner; but if intellect is the 'tool' of the will, as he says it is, then human actions are determined not by 'reason' but by 'will'. Eduard von Hartmann translated Schopenhauer's 'will' into 'the unconscious' (*The Philosophy of the Unconscious*, 1869, eight editions by 1879), and it is unnecessary to elaborate on what Freud subsequently made of 'the unconscious'. We are now so used to the notion that the springs of human conduct are to be sought not in the mind but in the 'will' that we have forgotten that this notion had to be invented, and consequently that it was Schopenhauer who invented it.

A fourth reason was the relative simplicity of his fundamental ideas. What chiefly contributed to the inaccessibility of philosophy was its historical method – its building on the philosophical past and its consequent demand for a great deal of knowledge of what had been thought and written before. The dominant philosophy during Schopenhauer's lifetime, that of Hegel, was especially exacting in this respect. Schopenhauer considered history of any kind unnecessary. 'To have read Herodotus is, from a philosophical point of view, to have studied enough history,' he wrote; and again, in direct riposte to Hegel: 'The true philosophy of history lies in perceiving that, in all the endless changes and motley complexity of events, it is only the self-same unchangeable being which is before us.' Instead of to history, Schopenhauer appealed to immediate experience, to the feelings and needs common to everyone, and it is about these that he is constantly writing. One result of this is that no German philosopher except Nietzsche employs less jargon: a few unavoidable and irreplaceable technical expressions whose meaning is easily learned suffice him.

Fifthly, there is the fact that Schopenhauer's literary style is a model of nineteenth-century German. No German philosopher had written so well or so readably before: he was not an innovator, but his manner was a faultless employment of the current idiom and demonstrated that the problems of metaphysics could be discussed in German in a way comprehensible to the non-specialist reader. Probably he was the first German philosopher to be read as 'literature' by a public not primarily interested in reading philosophy.

The ultimate ground of Schopenhauer's success, however, is that for many people he articulated a feeling hitherto inarticulate and therefore only half conscious that nineteenth-century progress was somehow not going to lead to the millennium. One has to try to think back to the time before the definitive collapse of that optimistic outlook which equated technological advance with human progress. No one with any sense will want to belittle the advantages of swift transportation, painless dentistry, refuse collection and all the other incalculably beneficial innovations of the nineteenth century; nor is it reasonable to expect of an age so incredibly prolific in practical inventions that it should have had a bad conscience about it. But we must also acknowledge that our civilization has now undergone a period of severe correction, so that optimism in nineteenth-century style would now be a kind of idiocy. Technological progress *may* still be going to lead to the millennium, but it could equally well lead to hell on earth. In 1818 however, and especially in Germany in 1818, the way things were going was hardly perceptible. Germany's advance into the industrial era was slow, a good generation behind that of England: early mercantile capitalism persisted well into the middle of the century. This explains why recognition of Schopenhauer was so long delayed: it came with the German rush into industrialization of the 1860s, 1870s and 1880s. The inauguration of the *Reich* was the beginning of an era of manic self-confidence which, by a natural process, produced its own antithesis: and it was only then that the great exponent and justifier of pessimism found his audience.

Publications

It will be convenient here to list the six books Schopenhauer published.

On the Fourfold Root of the Principle of Sufficient Reason, 1813; revised edition 1847. This is his doctoral thesis, later promoted to the 'first stage' of his philosophy.

On Vision and Colours, 1816; Latin version 1830. Goethe's largest scientific work was his three-volume *Zur Farbenlehre,* in which he expounded a theory of chromatics and polemicized against Newton's theory. Schopenhauer took sides with Goethe and published his own speculations on the subject. Characteristically, he preserved his support for Goethe and the enmity towards Newton he had learned from him until his last years.

The World as Will and Idea, 1818, dated 1819; second, much expanded edition 1844; third edition 1859.

On the Will in Nature, 1836; second edition 1854.

The Two Fundamental Problems of Ethics, 1841; second edition 1860.

Parerga and Paralipomena, 1851; various posthumous editions including additional notes and aphorisms.

Note on this Selection

The selection which follows is taken from the second volume of *Parerga and Paralipomena,* that is to say from the volume of aphorisms. The word is to be taken in the German sense, as meaning sometimes a single sentence but much more often a miniature essay on a single point. What I have called 'essays' are chains of aphorisms on a single subject. (Schopenhauer uses neither word: he calls the volume a collection of 'single but systematically ordered thoughts on diverse subjects'.) In making the selection I have been guided wholly and solely by what I thought interesting, either in itself or as a sample of Schopenhauer's way of thinking. Because it was assembled over many years the original collection is very repetitious: the same ideas occur again and again, and some pruning is justified quite apart

from the question of length. Much of Schopenhauer's speculation in the field of 'natural science' is now definitely antiquated
and I have had no qualms about omitting it (though a few
typical examples are retained as a matter of interest). Some of
his hobby horses – anti-vivisectionism and abuse of Hegel, for
instance – are ridden very hard: I have not hesitated to curb
them. Nor, once these to my mind necessary reductions had
been made, did there seem to be any logic in retaining the
original order of the aphorisms. The 'system' referred to in
Schopenhauer's subtitle consists solely in collecting the aphorisms together under chapter headings according to subject-
matter: the order of the chapters, while not exactly haphazard,
is in no way systematic. What I have done for the present selection is to reduce the original 31 chapter headings to 17 and then
to separate those chapters which constitute essays from those
which are collections of aphorisms.

January 1970   R.J.H.

ESSAYS

ON THE SUFFERING OF THE WORLD

1

IF the immediate and direct purpose of our life is not suffering then our existence is the most ill-adapted to its purpose in the world: for it is absurd to suppose that the endless affliction of which the world is everywhere full, and which arises out of the need and distress pertaining essentially to life, should be purposeless and purely accidental. Each individual misfortune, to be sure, seems an exceptional occurrence; but misfortune in general is the rule.

2

Just as a stream flows smoothly on as long as it encounters no obstruction, so the nature of man and animal is such that we never really notice or become conscious of what is agreeable to our will; if we are to notice something, our will has to have been thwarted, has to have experienced a shock of some kind. On the other hand, all that opposes, frustrates and resists our will, that is to say all that is unpleasant and painful, impresses itself upon us instantly, directly and with great clarity. Just as we are conscious not of the healthiness of our whole body but only of the little place where the shoe pinches, so we think not of the totality of our successful activities but of some insignificant trifle or other which continues to vex us. On this fact is founded what I have often before drawn attention to: the negativity of well-being and happiness, in antithesis to the positivity of pain.

I therefore know of no greater absurdity than that absurdity which characterizes almost all metaphysical systems: that of explaining evil as something negative. For evil is precisely that which is positive, that which makes itself palpable; and good, on the other hand, i.e. all happiness and all gratification, is that which is negative, the mere abolition of a desire and extinction of a pain.

This is also consistent with the fact that as a rule we find pleasure much less pleasurable, pain much more painful than we expected.

A quick test of the assertion that enjoyment outweighs pain in this world, or that they are at any rate balanced, would be to compare the feelings of an animal engaged in eating another with those of the animal being eaten.

3

The most effective consolation in every misfortune and every affliction is to observe others who are more unfortunate than we: and everyone can do this. But what does that say for the condition of the whole?

History shows us the life of nations and finds nothing to narrate but wars and tumults; the peaceful years appear only as occasional brief pauses and interludes. In just the same way the life of the individual is a constant struggle, and not merely a metaphorical one against want or boredom, but also an actual struggle against other people. He discovers adversaries everywhere, lives in continual conflict and dies with sword in hand.

4

Not the least of the torments which plague our existence is the constant pressure of *time*, which never lets us so much as draw breath but pursues us all like a taskmaster with a whip. It ceases to persecute only him it has delivered over to boredom.

5

And yet, just as our body would burst asunder if the pressure of the atmosphere were removed from it, so would the arrogance of men expand, if not to the point of bursting then to that of the most unbridled folly, indeed madness, if the pressure of want, toil, calamity and frustration were removed from their life. One can even say that we *require* at all times a certain quantity of care or sorrow or want, as a ship requires ballast, in order to keep on a straight course.

Work, worry, toil and trouble are indeed the lot of almost all men their whole life long. And yet if every desire were satisfied as soon as it arose how would men occupy their lives, how would they pass the time? Imagine this race transported to a Utopia where everything grows of its own accord and turkeys fly around ready-roasted, where lovers find one another without any delay and keep one another without any difficulty: in such a place some men would die of boredom or hang themselves, some would fight and kill one another, and thus they would create for themselves more suffering than nature inflicts on them as it is. Thus for a race such as this no stage, no form of existence is suitable other than the one it already possesses.

6

Since, as we recalled above, pleasure and well-being is negative and suffering positive, the happiness of a given life is not to be measured according to the joys and pleasures it contains but according to the absence of the positive element, the absence of suffering. This being so, however, the lot of the animals appears more endurable than that of man. Let us look at both a little more closely.

However varied the forms may be which human happiness and misery assume, inciting man to seek the one and flee from the other, the material basis of them all is physical pleasure or physical pain. This basis is very narrow: it consists of health, food, protection from wet and cold, and sexual gratification; or the lack of these things. Man has, consequently, no larger share of real physical pleasure than the animals have, except perhaps to the extent that his more highly charged nervous system intensifies every sensation of pleasure – as it also does every sensation of pain. Yet how much stronger are the emotions aroused in him than those aroused in the animals! how incomparably more profound and vehement are his passions! – and all to achieve exactly the same result in the end: health, food, covering, etc.

This arises first and foremost because with him everything is powerfully intensified by thinking about absent and future things, and this is in fact the origin of care, fear and hope, which, once they have been aroused, make a far stronger impression on men than do actual present pleasures or sufferings, to which the animal is limited. For, since it lacks the faculty of reflection, joys and sorrows cannot accumulate in the animal as they do in man through memory and anticipation. With the animal, present suffering, even if repeated countless times, remains what it was the first time: it cannot sum itself up. Hence the enviable composure and unconcern which characterizes the animal. With man, on the other hand, there evolves out of those elements of pleasure and suffering which he has in common with the animal an intensification of his sensations of happiness and misery which can lead to momentary transports which may sometimes even prove fatal, or to suicidal despair. More closely considered, what happens is this: he deliberately intensifies his needs, which are originally scarcely harder to satisfy than those of the animal, so as to intensify his pleasure: hence luxury, confectionery, tobacco, opium, alcoholic drinks, finery and all that pertains to them. To these is then added, also as a result of reflection, a source of pleasure, and consequently of suffering, available to him alone and one which preoccupies him beyond all measure, indeed more than all the rest put together: ambition and the sense of honour and shame – in plain words, what he thinks others think of him. This, in a thousand, often curious shapes then becomes the goal of all those endeavours of his which go beyond physical pleasure or pain. He excels the animal in his capacity for enjoying intellectual pleasures, to be sure, and these are available to him in many degrees, from the simplest jesting and conversation up to the highest achievements of the mind; but as a counterweight to this, on the side of suffering stands boredom, which is unknown to the animals at least in the state of nature and is only very slightly perceptible in the very cleverest domesticated ones, while to man it has become a veritable scourge. Want and boredom are indeed the twin poles of human life. Finally it remains to be mentioned that with man sexual gratification is tied to a very obstinate selectivity which is sometimes intensified into a more or less passionate love. Thus sexuality becomes for man a source of brief pleasure and protracted suffering.

It is indeed remarkable how, through the mere addition of thought, which the animal lacks, there should have been erected on the same narrow basis of pain and pleasure that the animal possesses so vast and lofty a structure of human happiness and misery, and man should be subjected to such vehement emotions, passions and convulsions that their impress can be read in enduring lines on his face; while all the time and in reality he is concerned only with the very same things which the animal too attains, and attains with an incomparably smaller expenditure of emotion. Through all this, however, the measure of suffering increases in man far more than the enjoyment, and it is very greatly enhanced specifically by the fact that he actually *knows* of death, while the animal only instinctively flees it without actually knowing of it and therefore without ever really having it in view, which man does all the time.

The animals are much more content with mere existence than we are; the plants are wholly so; and man is so according to how dull and insensitive he is. The animal's life consequently contains less suffering but also less pleasure than the human's, the direct reason being that on the one hand it is free from care and anxiety and the torments that attend them, but on the other is without hope and therefore has no share in that anticipation of a happy future which, together with the enchanting products of the imagination which accompany it, is the source of most of our greatest joys and pleasures. The animal lacks both anxiety and hope because its consciousness is restricted to what is clearly evident and thus to the present moment: the animal is the present incarnate. But precisely because this is so it appears in one respect to be truly sagacious compared with us, namely in its peaceful, untroubled enjoyment of the present: its obvious composure often puts to shame our own frequently restless and discontented condition.

7

If the above discussion has demonstrated that the reason man's life is more full of suffering than the animal's is his greater capacity for knowledge, we can now trace this back to a more general law and thus attain to a much more comprehensive view.

Knowledge is in itself always painless. Pain affects only the will and consists in an obstruction, impediment or frustration of it: nonetheless, this frustration of the will, if it is to be felt as pain, must be accompanied by knowledge. That is why even physical pain is conditioned by the nerves and their connexion with the brain, so that an injury to a limb is not felt if the nerves leading from the limb to the brain are severed or the brain itself is devitalized by chloroform. That spiritual pain is conditional upon knowledge goes without saying, and it is easy to see that it will increase with the degree of knowledge. We can thus express the whole relationship figuratively by saying that the will is the string, its frustration or impediment the vibration of the string, knowledge the sounding-board, and pain the sound.

Now this means that not only inorganic matter but the plant too is incapable of feeling pain, however many frustrations its will may undergo. On the other hand, every animal, even an *infusorium*, suffers pain, because knowledge, however imperfect, is the true characteristic of animality. At each higher stage of animal life there is a corresponding increase in pain. In the lowest animals it is extremely slight, but even in the highest it nowhere approaches the pain which man is capable of feeling, since even the highest animals lack thought and concepts. And it is right that this capacity for pain should reach its zenith only where, by virtue of the existence of reason, there also exists the possibility of denial of the will: for otherwise it would be nothing but aimless cruelty.

8

In our early youth we sit before the life that lies ahead of us like children sitting before the curtain in a theatre, in happy and tense anticipation of whatever is going to appear. Luckily we do not know what really will appear. For to him who does know, children can sometimes seem like innocent delinquents, sentenced not to death but to life, who have not yet discovered what their punishment will consist of. Nonetheless, everyone desires to achieve old age, that is to say a condition in which one can say: 'Today it is bad, and day by day it will get worse – until at last the worst of all arrives.'

9

If you imagine, in so far as it is approximately possible, the sum total of distress, pain and suffering of every kind which the sun shines upon in its course, you will have to admit it would have been much better if the sun had been able to call up the phenomenon of life as little on the earth as on the moon; and if, here as there, the surface were still in a crystalline condition.

You can also look upon our life as an episode unprofitably disturbing the blessed calm of nothingness. In any case, even he who has found life tolerably bearable will, the longer he lives, feel the more clearly that on the whole it is a disappointment, nay a cheat.[1] If two men who were friends in youth meet in old age after the lapse of an entire generation, the principal feeling the sight of one another, linked as it is with recollections of earlier years, will arouse in both will be one of total disappointment with the whole of life, which once lay so fair before them in the rosy dawn of youth, promised so much and performed so little. This feeling will dominate so decidedly over every other that they will not even think it necessary to speak of it but will silently assume it as the basis of their conversation.

If the act of procreation were neither the outcome of a desire nor accompanied by feelings of pleasure, but a matter to be decided on the basis of purely rational considerations, is it likely

1. The last four words are in English in the original.

the human race would still exist? Would each of us not rather have felt so much pity for the coming generation as to prefer to spare it the burden of existence, or at least not wish to take it upon himself to impose that burden upon it in cold blood?

For the world is Hell, and men are on the one hand the tormented souls and on the other the devils in it.

Brahma is supposed to have created the world by a kind of fall into sin, or by an error, and has to atone for this sin or error by remaining in it himself until he has redeemed himself out of it. Very good! In *Buddhism* the world arises as a consequence of an inexplicable clouding of the heavenly clarity of the blessed state of Nirvana after a long period of quietude. Its origin is thus a kind of fatality which is fundamentally to be understood in a moral sense, notwithstanding the case has an exact analogy in the physical world in the origin of the sun in an inexplicable primeval streak of mist. Subsequently, however, as a consequence of moral misdeeds it gradually deteriorates physically too, until it has assumed its present sad condition. Excellent! To the *Greeks* the world and the gods were the work of an unfathomable necessity: that will do as a provisional explanation. *Ormuzd* is continually at war with *Ahriman*: that is worth considering.[2] But that a god like *Jehovah* should create this world of want and misery *animi causa*[3] and *de gaieté de cœur* and then go so far as to applaud himself for it, saying it is all very good: that is quite unacceptable.

Even if Leibniz's demonstration that this is the best of all *possible* worlds were correct, it would still not be a vindication of divine providence. For the Creator created not only the world, he also created possibility itself: therefore he should have created the possibility of a better world than this one.

In general, however, two things cry out against any such view of the world as the successful work of an infinitely wise, infinitely good and at the same time infinitely powerful being: the misery of which it is full and the obvious imperfection of its

2. Brahma is the principal deity of Hinduism. Ormuzd is the good God, Ahriman the bad God of Zoroastrianism, the ancient religion of Persia.

3. Capriciously, voluntarily.

most highly developed phenomenon, man, who is indeed a grotesque caricature. This is a dissonance that cannot be resolved. On the contrary, it is precisely these instances which support what we have been saying and which provide evidence for our conception of the world as the product of our own sins and therefore as something that had better not have been. Under the former conception they become a bitter indictment of the Creator and supply material for cynicisms, while under our conception they appear as an indictment of our own nature and will, and one calculated to teach us humility. For they lead us to the insight that, like the children of libertine fathers, we come into the world already encumbered with guilt and that it is only because we have continually to atone for this guilt that our existence is so wretched and its end is death. Nothing is more certain than that, generally speaking, it is the grievous *sin of the world* which gives rise to the manifold and great *suffering of the world*; whereby is meant not any physical-empirical connexion but a metaphysical one. The story of the Fall is consequently the only thing which reconciles me to the Old Testament; I even regard it as the sole metaphysical truth contained in that book, even though it does appear clothed in allegory. For our existence resembles nothing so much as the consequence of a misdeed, punishment for a forbidden desire.

As a reliable compass for orientating yourself in life nothing is more useful than to accustom yourself to regarding this world as a place of atonement, a sort of penal colony. When you have done this you will order your expectations of life according to the nature of things and no longer regard the calamities, sufferings, torments and miseries of life as something irregular and not to be expected but will find them entirely in order, well knowing that each of us is here being punished for his existence and each in his own particular way. This outlook will enable us to view the so-called imperfections of the majority of men, i.e. their moral and intellectual shortcomings and the facial appearance resulting therefrom, without surprise and certainly without indignation: for we shall always bear in mind where we are and consequently regard every man first and foremost as a being who exists only as a consequence of his culpability and whose life is an expiation of the crime of being born.

The conviction that the world, and therefore man too, is something which really ought not to exist is in fact calculated to instil in us indulgence towards one another: for what can be expected of beings placed in such a situation as we are? From this point of view one might indeed consider that the appropriate form of address between man and man ought to be, not *monsieur, sir*, but *fellow sufferer, compagnon de misères*. However strange this may sound it corresponds to the nature of the case, makes us see other men in a true light and reminds us of what are the most necessary of all things: tolerance, patience, forbearance and charity, which each of us needs and which each of us therefore owes.

ON THE VANITY OF EXISTENCE

I

THE vanity of existence is revealed in the whole form existence assumes: in the infiniteness of time and space contrasted with the finiteness of the individual in both; in the fleeting present as the sole form in which actuality exists; in the contingency and relativity of all things; in continual becoming without being; in continual desire without satisfaction; in the continual frustration of striving of which life consists. *Time* and that *perishability* of all things existing in time that time itself brings about is simply the form under which the will to live, which as thing in itself is imperishable, reveals to itself the vanity of its striving. Time is that by virtue of which everything becomes nothingness in our hands and loses all real value.

2

That which *has been* no longer *is*; it as little exists as does that which has *never* been. But everything that *is* in the next moment *has been*. Thus the most insignificant present has over the most significant past the advantage of *actuality*, which means that the former bears to the latter the relation of something to nothing.

To our amazement we suddenly exist, after having for countless millennia not existed; in a short while we will again not exist, also for countless millennia. That cannot be right, says the heart: and even upon the crudest intelligence there must, when it considers such an idea, dawn a presentiment of the ideality of time. This however, together with that of space, is the key to all true metaphysics, because it makes room for a quite different order of things than that of nature. That is why Kant is so great.

Every moment of our life belongs to the present only for a moment; then it belongs for ever to the past. Every evening we are poorer by a day. We would perhaps grow frantic at the sight of this ebbing away of our short span of time were we not secretly conscious in the profoundest depths of our being that we share in the inexhaustible well of eternity, out of which we can for ever draw new life and renewed time.

You could, to be sure, base on considerations of this kind a theory that the greatest *wisdom* consists in enjoying the present and making this enjoyment the goal of life, because the present is all that is real and everything else merely imaginary. But you could just as well call this mode of life the greatest *folly*: for that which in a moment ceases to exist, which vanishes as completely as a dream, cannot be worth any serious effort.

3

Our existence has no foundation on which to rest except the transient present. Thus its form is essentially unceasing *motion*, without any possibility of that repose which we continually strive after. It resembles the course of a man running down a mountain who would fall over if he tried to stop and can stay on his feet only by running on; or a pole balanced on the tip of the finger; or a planet which would fall into its sun if it ever ceased to plunge irresistibly forward. Thus existence is typified by unrest.

In such a world, where no stability of any kind, no enduring state is possible, where everything is involved in restless change and confusion and keeps itself on its tightrope only by continually striding forward – in such a world, happiness is not so much as to be thought of. It cannot dwell where nothing occurs but Plato's 'continual becoming and never being'. In the first place, no man is happy but strives his whole life long after a supposed happiness which he seldom attains, and even if he does it is only to be disappointed with it; as a rule, however, he finally enters harbour shipwrecked and dismasted. In the second place, however, it is all one whether he has been happy or not in a life which has consisted merely of a succession of transient present moments and is now at an end.

4

The scenes of our life resemble pictures in rough mosaic; they are ineffective from close up, and have to be viewed from a distance if they are to seem beautiful. That is why to attain something desired is to discover how vain it is; and why, though we live all our lives in expectation of better things, we often at the same time long regretfully for what is past. The present, on the other hand, is regarded as something quite temporary and serving only as the road to our goal. That is why most men discover when they look back on their life that they have the whole time been living *ad interim*, and are surprised to see that which they let go by so unregarded and unenjoyed was precisely their life, was precisely that in expectation of which they lived.

5

Life presents itself first and foremost as a task: the task of maintaining itself, *de gagner sa vie*. If this task is accomplished, what has been gained is a burden, and there then appears a second task: that of doing something with it so as to ward off boredom, which hovers over every secure life like a bird of prey. Thus the first task is to gain something and the second to become unconscious of what has been gained, which is otherwise a burden.

That human life must be some kind of mistake is sufficiently proved by the simple observation that man is a compound of needs which are hard to satisfy; that their satisfaction achieves nothing but a painless condition in which he is only given over to boredom; and that boredom is a direct proof that existence is in itself valueless, for boredom is nothing other than the sensation of the emptiness of existence. For if life, in the desire for which our essence and existence consists, possessed in itself a positive value and real content, there would be no such thing as boredom: mere existence would fulfil and satisfy us. As things are, we take no pleasure in existence except when we are striving after something – in which case distance and difficulties make our goal look as if it would satisfy us (an illusion which fades when we reach it) – or when engaged in purely intellectual activity, in which case we are really stepping out of life so as to regard it from outside, like spectators at a play. Even sensual pleasure itself consists in a continual striving and ceases as soon as its goal is reached. Whenever we are not involved in one or other of these things but directed back to existence itself we are overtaken by its worthlessness and vanity and this is the sensation called boredom.

6

That the most perfect manifestation of the will to live represented by the human organism, with its incomparably ingenious and complicated machinery, must crumble to dust and its whole essence and all its striving be palpably given over at last to annihilation – this is nature's unambiguous declaration that all the striving of this will is essentially vain. If it were something possessing value in itself, something which ought unconditionally to exist, it would not have non-being as its goal.

Yet what a difference there is between our beginning and our end! We begin in the madness of carnal desire and the transport of voluptuousness, we end in the dissolution of all our parts and the musty stench of corpses. And the road from the one to the other too goes, in regard to our well-being and enjoyment of life, steadily downhill: happily dreaming childhood, exultant youth, toil-filled years of manhood, infirm and often wretched old age, the torment of the last illness and finally the throes of death – does it not look as if existence were an error the consequences of which gradually grow more and more manifest?

We shall do best to think of life as a *desengaño*, as a process of disillusionment: since this is, clearly enough, what everything that happens to us is calculated to produce.

ON THE ANTITHESIS OF THING IN
ITSELF AND APPEARANCE

1

THING in itself signifies that which exists independently of our perception, that which actually is. To Democritus it was matter; fundamentally this is what it still was to Locke; to Kant it was = x; to me it is *will*.[1]

2

Just as we know of the earth only the surface, not the great, solid masses of the interior, so we know empirically of things and the world nothing at all except their *appearances*, i.e. the surface. Exact knowledge of this constitutes *physics*, taken in the widest sense. But that this surface presupposes an interior which is not merely superficies but possesses cubic content is, together with deductions as to the character of this interior, the theme of *metaphysics*. To seek to construe the nature of things in themselves according to the laws of appearance is an undertaking to be compared with seeking to construe stereometric bodies out of superficies and the laws that apply to them. Every *dogmatic transcendental* philosophy is an attempt to construe the *thing in itself* according to the laws of *appearance*, which is like trying to make two absolutely dissimilar bodies cover one another, an attempt which always fails because however you may turn them this or that corner always protrudes.

1. Democritus (*fl. c.* 420 B.C.), Greek philosopher, the founder of atomism. John Locke (1632–1704), the representative British philosopher of the late seventeenth century.

3

Because everything in nature is at once *appearance* and *thing in itself*, or *natura naturata* and *natura naturans*, it is consequently susceptible of a twofold explanation, a *physical* and a *metaphysical*. The physical explanation is always in terms of *cause*, the metaphysical in terms of *will*; for that which appears in cognitionless nature as *natural force*, and on a higher level as *life force*, receives in animal and man the name *will*. Strictly speaking, therefore, the degree and tendency of a man's intelligence and the constitution of his moral character could perhaps be traced back to purely *physical* causes, the former from the constitution of his brain and nervous system, together with the blood circulation which affects them, the latter from the constitution and combined effect of his heart, vascular system, blood, lungs, liver, spleen, kidneys, intestines, genitalia, etc.; which would, I grant, demand a much more exact knowledge of the laws governing the *rapport du physique au moral* than even Bichat and Cabanis possessed.[2] Both could then be further traced back to their more remote physical cause, namely the constitution of his parents, inasmuch as these could furnish the seed only for a similar being and not for one higher or better. *Metaphysically*, on the other hand, the same man would have to be explained as the apparitional form of his own, utterly free and primal will, which has created for itself the intellect appropriate to it; so that all his actions, however necessarily they may be the result of his character in conflict with the motivations acting on him at any given time, and however necessarily these again may arise as a consequence of his corporeity, are nonetheless to be attributed wholly to him.

4

When we perceive and consider the existence, life and activity of any natural creature, e.g. an animal, it stands before us, every-

2. Marie François Xavier Bichat (1771–1802), anatomist and physiologist. Pierre Jean Georges Cabanis (1757–1808), physician and writer on medicine.

thing zoology and zootomy teaches notwithstanding, as an unfathomable mystery. But must nature then, from sheer obduracy, for ever remain dumb to our questioning? Is nature not, as everything great is, open, communicative and even naïve? Can her failure to reply ever be for any other reason than that we have asked the wrong question, that our question has been based on false presuppositions, that it has even harboured a contradiction? For can it be imagined that a connexion between causes and consequences could exist in nature which is essentially and for ever undiscoverable? – No, certainly not. Nature is unfathomable because we seek after causes and consequences in a realm where this form is not to be found. We try to reach the inner being of nature, which looks out at us from every phenomenon, under the guidance of the principle of sufficient reason – whereas this is merely the form under which our intellect comprehends appearance, i.e. the surface of things, while we want to employ it beyond the bounds of appearance; for within these bounds it is serviceable and sufficient. Here, for example, the existence of a given animal can be explained by its procreation. This is fundamentally no more mysterious than the issuing of any other effect, even the simplest, from its cause, inasmuch as even in the simplest case the explanation finally strikes the incomprehensible. That in the case of procreation we lack a couple more stages in the causal connexion makes no essential difference, for even if we had them we should still stand at last before the incomprehensible, because appearance remains appearance and does not become thing in itself.

5

We complain of the darkness in which we live out our lives: we do not understand the nature of existence in general; we especially do not know the relation of our own self to the rest of existence. Not only is our life short, our knowledge is limited entirely to it, since we can see neither back before our birth nor out beyond our death, so that our consciousness is as it were a lightning-flash momentarily illuminating the night: it truly seems as though a demon had maliciously shut off all further knowledge from us so as to enjoy our discomfiture.

But this complaint is not really justified: for it arises out of an illusion produced by the false premise that the totality of things proceeded from an *intellect* and consequently existed as an *idea* before it became actual; according to which premise the totality of things, having arisen from the realm of knowledge, must be entirely accessible to knowledge and entirely explicable and capable of being exhaustively comprehended by it. – But the truth of the matter is, I fear, that all that of which we complain of not knowing is not known to anyone, indeed is probably as such unknowable, i.e. not capable of being conceived.[3] For the *idea*, in whose domain all knowledge lies and to which all knowledge therefore refers, is only the outer side of existence, something secondary, supplementary, something, that is, which was necessary not for the preservation of things as such, the universal totality, but merely for the preservation of the individual animal being. Consequently the existence of things as a whole entered into the realm of knowledge only *per accidens*, thus to a very limited extent: it forms only the background of the painting in the animal consciousness, where the objectives of the will are the essential element and occupy the front rank. There then arose through this *accidens* the entire world of space and time, i.e. the world as idea, which possesses no existence of this sort at all outside the realm of knowledge. Now since knowledge exists only for the purpose of preserving each animal individual, its whole constitution, all its forms, such as time, space, etc., are adapted merely to the aims of such an individual: and these require knowledge only of relations between individual phenomena and by no means knowledge of the essential nature of things and the universal totality.

Kant has demonstrated that the problems of metaphysics which trouble everyone to a greater or less degree are capable of no direct solution and of no satisfactory solution at all. The

3. *Nicht vorstellbar*: not imaginable or conceivable; but in Schopenhauer's usage also bearing the more specific sense of 'not able to be a *Vorstellung*, an *idea*'.

reason for this is ultimately that they have their origin in the forms of our intellect – time, space and causality – while this intellect is designed merely to prescribe to the individual will its motivations, i.e. to indicate to it the objectives of its desires, together with the means of taking possession of them. But if this intellect is abused by being directed upon the being in itself of things, upon the totality and the inner constitution of the world, then the aforesaid forms of the contiguity, successiveness and interdependence of all possible things give birth to metaphysical problems such as those of the origin and purpose, the beginning and end of the world and of one's own self, of the annihilation of this through death or its continued existence in spite of death, of freedom of will, and so forth. If we imagine these forms for once removed, however, and a consciousness of things nonetheless still present, then these problems would be, not solved, but non-existent: they would utterly vanish, and the sentences expressing them would no longer have any meaning. For they arise entirely out of these forms, whose object is not an understanding of the world and existence, but merely an understanding of our own aims.

This whole way of looking at the question offers us an explanation and *objective* proof of the Kantian theory, which its originator proved only from the *subjective* point of view, that the forms of reason can be employed only immanently, not transcendentally. For instead of putting it in this manner one could say: the intellect is physical not metaphysical, i.e. since, as appertaining to the will's objectivization it originates in the will, it exists only to serve the will: this service, however, concerns only things *in* nature, and not things lying outside and beyond nature. It is obvious that an animal possesses intellect only for the purpose of discovering and capturing its food; the degree of intellect it possesses is determined by this purpose. It is no different in the case of man; except that here the greater difficulty of preserving and maintaining him and the endless augmentability of his needs has made necessary a much greater degree of intellect. Only when this is exceeded through an abnormality does there appear a *superfluity of intellect exempt from service*: when this superfluity becomes considerable it is called *genius*. Such an intellect will first of all become *objective*, but it can even go on to become to a certain degree metaphysical, or at least strive to become so: for the consequence of its objectivity is that nature itself, the totality of things, now becomes the intellect's subject-matter and problem. In such an intellect nature first begins properly to perceive itself as something which is and yet could *not* be, or could be *other* than it is; whereas in the ordinary, merely normal intellect nature does not clearly perceive itself – just as the miller does not hear his own mill or the perfumer smell his own shop. To the normal intellect nature appears simply as a matter of course: it is caught up in and encompassed by nature. Only in certain more luminous moments will it perceive nature and it is then almost terrified at the sight: but the feeling soon passes. What such normal heads can achieve in philosophy, even if they crowd together in their thousands, is consequently easy to imagine; but if intellect were metaphysical, in its origin and in its vocation, it could promote philosophy, especially if its forces were united, as well as it can promote every other science.

ON AFFIRMATION AND DENIAL
OF THE WILL TO LIVE

1

IT is to some extent obvious *a priori – vulgo* it goes without saying – that that which at present produces the phenomenon of the world must be capable of not doing so and consequently remaining inactive. Now if the former state constitutes the phenomenon of the volition of life, the latter will constitute the phenomenon of non-volition. And this will be in its essence identical with the *Magnum Sakhepat* of the Vedanta and the Nirvana of the Buddhists.

The denial of the will to live does not in any way imply the annihilation of a substance; it means merely the act of non-volition: that which previously *willed*, *wills* no more. This *will*, as thing in itself, is known to us only in and through the act of *volition*, and we are therefore incapable of saying or of conceiving what it is or does further after it has ceased to perform this act: thus this denial of the will to live is *for us*, who are phenomena of volition, a transition to nothingness.

2

Between the ethics of the Greeks and those of the Hindus there exists a glaring antithesis. The object of the former (though with Plato excepted) is to make it possible to lead a happy life, a *vitam beatam*, that of the latter, on the contrary, to liberate and redeem from life altogether, as is directly stated in the very first sentence of the *Sankhya Karika*.

You perceive a similar contrast – a contrast strengthened by its being in visible form – if you regard the beautiful antique sarcophagus in the gallery at Florence on which is depicted in relief the entire ceremonial of a wedding, from the first proposal to the point where Hymen's torch lights the way to the bridal chamber, and then compare it with a *Christian* coffin, draped in black as a sign of mourning and with a crucifix upon it. The antithesis is in the highest degree significant. Both desire to offer consolation in face of death; they do so in opposite ways, and both are right. The one expresses *affirmation* of the will to life, through which life is assured for all time, however swiftly its figures and forms may succeed one another. The other, by symbols of suffering and death, expresses *denial* of the will to life and redemption from a world in which death and the Devil reign. Between the spirit of Graeco-Roman paganism and the spirit of Christianity the real antithesis is that of affirmation and denial of the will to live – in which regard Christianity is in the last resort fundamentally in the right.

3

My ethics stands in the same relation to that of all other European philosophers as the New Testament does to the Old, taking this relationship in the ecclesiastical sense. For the Old Testament places man under the dominion of the Law, which Law, however, does not lead to redemption. The New Testament, on the other hand, declares that the Law is insufficient and, indeed, absolves man from obedience to it.[1] In its place it preaches the kingdom of grace, which one can enter through faith, charity and total denial of self: this, it says, is the road to redemption from evil and from the world: for – every Protestant and Rationalist misrepresentation notwithstanding – the true soul of the New Testament is undoubtedly the spirit of asceticism. This spirit of asceticism is precisely denial of the will to live, and the transition from the Old Testament to the New, from the dominion of the Law to the dominion of faith, from justification by works to redemption through the Intercessor, from the dominion of sin and death to eternal life in Christ, signifies, *sensu proprio*, the transition from merely moral virtue to denial of the will to live. All philosophical ethics before me cleaves to

1. Schopenhauer cites Romans vii and Galatians ii and iii.

the spirit of the Old Testament: it posits an absolute moral law (i.e. one which has no foundation and no goal) and consists of moral commandments and prohibitions behind which a dictatorial Jehovah is silently introduced; and this is true however different the forms may be in which this ethical philosophy appears. My ethics, on the contrary, possesses foundation, aim and goal: first and foremost, it demonstrates theoretically the metaphysical foundation of justice and charity, and then indicates the goal to which these, if practised in perfection, must ultimately lead. At the same time it candidly confesses the reprehensible nature of the world and points to the denial of the will as the road to redemption from it. My ethics is thus actually in the spirit of the New Testament, while all the others are in that of the Old and consequently amount, even theoretically, to nothing more than Judaism, which is to say naked, despotic theism. In this sense my doctrine could be called the true Christian philosophy, however paradoxical this may seem to those who refuse to penetrate to the heart of the matter but prefer its superficialities.

4

He who is capable of thinking a little more deeply will soon perceive that human desires cannot begin to be sinful simply at that point at which, in their chance encounters with one another, they occasion harm and evil; but that, if this is what they bring about, they must be originally and in their essence sinful and reprehensible, and the entire will to live itself reprehensible. All the cruelty and torment of which the world is full is in fact merely the necessary result of the totality of the forms under which the will to live is objectified, and thus merely a commentary on the affirmation of the will to live. That our existence itself implies guilt is proved by the fact of death.

5

If in comprehending the world you start from the thing in itself, from the will to live, you discover that its kernel, its point of greatest concentration, is the act of generation. What a contrast, on the other hand, is presented if you start from the world of appearance, the empirical world, the world as idea! Here the act of generation is seen as something completely detached and distinct, of subordinate importance, indeed as something secondary to be veiled and hidden, as a paradoxical anomaly offering plentiful material for humour. It might occur to us, however, that this is only a case of the Devil's concealing his game: for has it not been noticed that sexual desire, especially when concentrated into infatuation through fixation on a particular woman, is the quintessence of this noble world's imposture, since it promises so excessively much and performs so miserably little?

The woman's part in procreation is in a certain sense more innocent than the man's, inasmuch as the man gives to the child *will*, which is the prime sin and thus the source of all wickedness and evil, while the woman gives it *knowledge*, which opens the road to salvation. The act of generation is the node of the universe; it declares: 'The will to live is once more affirmed.' Conception and pregnancy, on the other hand, declare: 'To the will there is once more joined the light of knowledge' – by means of which it can find its way out of the world again and the possibility of redemption is thus once more opened up.

It is this which explains the notable fact that every woman, while she would be ready to die of shame if surprised in the act of generation, nonetheless carries her pregnancy without a trace of shame and indeed with a kind of pride. The reason is that pregnancy is in a certain sense a cancellation of the guilt incurred by coitus: thus coitus bears all the shame and disgrace of the affair, while pregnancy, which is so intimately associated with it, stays pure and innocent and is indeed to some extent sacred.

Coitus is chiefly an affair of the man, pregnancy entirely that of the woman. The child receives from its father will and character, from its mother intellect. The latter is the redeeming principle, the will the principle of bondage. Coitus is the sign that, despite every increase in illumination through the intellect, the will to live continues to exist in time; the renewed incarnation of the will to live is the sign that the light of knowledge, and that in the highest degree of clarity, the possibility of redemption, has again been joined to this will. The sign of this is pregnancy, which therefore goes about frankly and freely, indeed with pride, while coitus hides itself away like a criminal.

6

Unjust or wicked actions are, in regard to him who performs them, signs of the strength of his affirmation of the will to live, and thus of how far he still is from true salvation, which is denial of this will, and from redemption from the world; they are also signs of how long a schooling in knowledge and suffering he still has to undergo before he can attain it. In regard to him who has to suffer these actions, however, although physically they are an evil, metaphysically they are a good and fundamentally beneficial, since they assist him along the road to his true salvation.

7

World Spirit This then is the task of all your labour and all your suffering: it is for this that you *exist,* as all other things exist.

Man But what do I get from existence? If it is full I have only distress, if empty only boredom. How can you offer me so poor a reward for so much labour and so much suffering?

World Spirit And yet it is proportionate to all your toil and all your suffering, and is so precisely on account of its meagreness.

Man Indeed! That passes my comprehension.

World Spirit I know it does. – (*Aside*) Should I tell him that the value of life lies precisely in this, that it teaches him not to want it? For this supreme initiation life itself must prepare him.

ON THE INDESTRUCTIBILITY OF OUR
ESSENTIAL BEING BY DEATH

I

You should read Jean Paul's *Selina* to see how a mind of the first order tries to deal with what he comes to think nonsensical in a false concept which he does not want to relinquish because he has set his heart upon it, although he is continually troubled by absurdities he cannot stomach.[1] The concept in question is that of the continued individual existence of our entire personal consciousness after death. This struggling and wrestling on the part of Jean Paul shows that ideas of this kind, compounded of true and false concepts, are not, as is generally thought, fruitful errors but rather decidedly harmful ones: for the false antithesis between soul and body and the elevation of the total personality to a thing in itself which must endure for ever makes it impossible to arrive at a true knowledge, deriving from the antithesis between appearance and thing in itself, of the indestructibility of our intrinsic being as something unaffected by time, causality and change; moreover, this false concept cannot even be held on to as a surrogate of truth, because reason continually rebels at the absurdity contained in it and is then obliged also to relinquish the truth amalgamated with it. For truth can in the long run endure only in a pure state: tempered with error, it partakes of the frailty of error.

1. Johannes Paul Friedrich Richter (1763–1825), known by his pen-name of Jean Paul, was one of the most popular German writers of his age. *Selina*, published posthumously in 1827, is an unsuccessful attempt to think clearly what his religious beliefs actually amount to: Jean Paul decides he cannot accept Christianity, but finds it impossible to surrender a number of beliefs, e.g. the belief in immortality, of which he could never have had any conception except as constituents of the Christian religion he rejects.

2

If, in everyday life, you are asked about continued existence after death by one of those people who would like to know everything but refuse to learn anything, the most appropriate and approximately correct reply is: 'After your death you will be what you were before your birth.' For this answer implies that it is preposterous to demand that a species of existence which had a beginning should not have an end; in addition, however, it contains a hint that there may be two kinds of existence and, correspondingly, two kinds of nothingness. You might, however, also reply: 'Whatever you will be after your death – even though it were nothing – will then be just as natural and suitable to you as your individual organic existence is now: thus the most you have to fear is the moment of transition. Indeed, since mature consideration of the matter leads to the conclusion that total non-being would be preferable to such an existence as ours is, the idea of the cessation of our existence, or of a time in which we no longer are, can from a rational point of view trouble us as little as the idea that we had never been. Now since this existence is essentially a personal one, the ending of the personality cannot be regarded as a loss.'

3

If we imagine a creature which surveys, knows and understands everything, then the question whether we exist after death would for that creature probably have no meaning, because outside of our present temporal, individual state of being, existence and cessation would no longer signify anything, but would be concepts indistinguishable from one another; so that neither the concept of destruction nor that of continued existence could be applied to our intrinsic and essential being, the thing in itself, of which we are the phenomenal appearance, since these concepts are borrowed from the realm of time, which is merely the form of phenomena. On the other hand, we can imagine the *indestructibility* of this kernel of our phenomenal appearance only as its *continued existence*, and indeed intrinsically only according to the scheme of the *material world*, as which it remains, with all its changes of form, firmly lodged in time. If, now, this kernel is denied its continued existence, we regard our temporal end as an annihilation, according to the scheme of the *form*, which disappears when the material which bears it is withdrawn. Both ideas are, however, a transference of the forms of the phenomenal world on to the thing in itself. But of an indestructibility which is not a continued existence we can hardly construct even an abstract conception, because we lack every intuition for doing so.

In truth, however, the continual coming into existence of new beings and the annihilation of already existing ones is to be regarded as an illusion produced by a contrivance of two lenses (brain-functions) through which alone we can see anything at all: they are called space and time, and in their interpenetration causality. For everything we perceive under these conditions is merely phenomenon; we do not know what things are like in themselves, i.e. independently of our perception of them. This is the actual kernel of the Kantian philosophy.

4

How can one believe that when a human being *dies* a thing in itself has come *to nothing*? Mankind knows, directly and intuitively, that when this happens it is only a phenomenon coming to an end in time, the form of all phenomena, without the thing in itself being affected thereby. We all feel that we are something other than a being which someone once created out of nothing: from this arises the confidence that, while death may be able to end our life, it cannot end our existence.

5

The more clearly you become conscious of the frailty, vanity and dream-like quality of all things, the more clearly will you also become conscious of the eternity of your own inner being;

because it is only in contrast to this that the aforesaid quality of things becomes evident, just as you perceive the speed at which a ship is going only when looking at the motionless shore, not when looking into the ship itself.

6

The *present* has two halves: an *objective* and a *subjective*. The objective half alone has the intuition of *time* as its form and thus streams irresistibly away; the subjective half stands firm and thus is always the same. It is from this that there originates our lively recollection of what is long past and, despite our knowledge of the fleetingness of our existence, the consciousness of our immortality.

Whenever we may live we always stand, with our consciousness, at the central point of time, never at its termini, and we may deduce from that that each of us bears within him the unmoving mid-point of the whole of endless time. It is fundamentally this which gives us the confidence to live without being in continual dread of death.

He who, by virtue of the strength of his memory and imagination, can most clearly call up what is long past in his own life will be more conscious than others of the *identity of all present moments throughout the whole of time*. Through this consciousness of the identity of all present moments one apprehends that which is most fleeting of all, the moment, as that alone which persists. And he who, in such intuitive fashion, becomes aware that the *present*, which is in the strictest sense the sole form of reality, has its source *in us*, and thus arises from within and not from without, cannot doubt the indestructibility of his own being. He will understand, rather, that although when he dies the objective world, with the medium through which it presents itself, the intellect, will be lost to him, his existence will not be affected by it; for there has been as much reality within him as without.

Whoever does not acknowledge all this will be obliged to assert the opposite and say: 'Time is something completely objective and real which exists quite independently of me. I was only thrown into it by chance, have taken possession of a little of it and thereby attained to an ephemeral reality, as thousands of others who are now nothing have done before me, and I too shall very soon be nothing. Time, on the other hand, is what is real: it will then go on without me.' I think the fundamental perversity, indeed absurdity, of this view has only to be clearly stated to become obvious.

All this means, to be sure, that life can be regarded as a dream and death as the awakening from it: but it must be remembered that the personality, the individual, belongs to the dreaming and not to the awakened consciousness, which is why death appears to the individual as annihilation. In any event, death is not, from this point of view, to be considered a transition to a state completely new and foreign to us, but rather a return to one originally our own from which life has been only a brief absence.

Consciousness is destroyed in death, to be sure; but that which has been producing it is by no means destroyed. For consciousness depends first of all on the intellect, but the intellect depends on a physiological process: it is obviously the function of the brain and is thus conditioned by the collaboration of the nervous and vascular systems; more precisely, by the brain nourished, animated and constantly stimulated by the heart; the brain through whose ingenious and mysterious structure, which anatomy can describe but physiology cannot understand, there come about the phenomena of the objective world and the workings of our thoughts. An individual consciousness, that is to say a consciousness of any kind, cannot be thought of apart from a *corporeal being*, because cognition, which is the precondition of all consciousness, is necessarily a function of the brain – properly speaking because brain is the objective form of intellect. Now since intellect appears physiologically, and consequently in empirical reality, i.e. in the realm of phenomenon, as something secondary, as a result of the life-process, it is also secondary psychologically, in antithesis to will, which alone is primary and everywhere the original element. And since, therefore, consciousness does not adhere directly to will but is conditioned by intellect, and this last is conditioned by the organism, there can be no doubt that consciousness is extinguished by death – as it is by sleep or by any form of fainting or swoon. But cheer up! – for what kind of a consciousness is it? A cerebral, an animal, a somewhat more highly charged bestial consciousness, in as far as we have it in all essentials in common with the whole animal world, even if it does reach its peak in us. This consciousness is, in its origin and aim, merely an expedient for helping the animal to get what it needs. The state to which death restores us, on the other hand, is our original state, i.e. is the being's intrinsic state, the moving principle of which appears in the production and maintenance of the life which is now coming to an end : it is the state of the thing in itself, in antithesis to the world of appearance. And in this primal state such a makeshift as cerebral, highly mediate cognition, which precisely because it is so is cognition only of phenomena, is altogether superfluous; which is precisely why we lose it. For us its abolition is one with the cessation of the world of phenomena whose mere medium it was and in which capacity alone it is of any use. Even if in this primal state we were offered the retention of this animal consciousness we should reject it, as the cured cripple rejects his crutch. Whoever therefore regrets the impending loss of this cerebral consciousness, which is adapted to and capable of producing only phenomena, is to be compared with the converts from Greenland who refused to go to Heaven when they learned there would be no seals there.

Everything said here rests, further, on the presupposition that *we* can imagine a state which is *not unconscious* only as one which is *cognisant* and moreover bears the stamp of the basic form of all cognition, the division into subject and object, into that which knows and that which is known : but we have to consider that this whole form of knowing and being known is conditioned merely by our animal nature, which is moreover very secondary and derivative, and is thus by no means the primal state of all essential being and existence, which may therefore be quite differently constituted and yet *not unconscious*.

Our intrinsic actual being is, so far as we are able to penetrate it, nothing but *will,* and this is in itself without cognition. If, then, death deprives us of intellect we are thereby only transported to our *cognitionless* primal state, which is not however simply an *unconscious* state but rather one elevated above that form, a state in which the antithesis of subject and object falls away, because that which is to be known would here be actually and undividedly one with that which knows and the basic condition of all cognition (which is precisely this antithesis) would be lacking.

7

If now, instead of looking *inwards*, we again look *outwards* and take an objective view of the world which presents itself to us, then death will certainly appear to us as a transition into nothingness; on the other hand, however, birth will appear as a coming forth out of nothingness. But neither the one nor the other can be unconditionally true, for they possess the reality only of the phenomenal world. And that we should in some sense or other survive death is no greater miracle than that of procreation, which we have before our eyes every day. What dies goes to where all life originates, its own included. From this point of view our life is to be regarded as a loan received from death, with sleep as the daily interest on this loan. Death announces itself frankly as the end of the individual, but in this individual there lies the germ of a new being. Thus nothing that dies dies for ever; but nothing that is born receives a fundamentally new existence. That which dies is destroyed; but a germ remains over out of which there proceeds a new being, which then enters into existence without knowing whence it has come nor why it is as it is. This is the mystery of *palingenesis*; it reveals to us that all those beings living at the present moment contain within them the actual germ of all which will live in the future, and that these therefore in a certain sense exist already. So that every animal in the full prime of life seems to call to us: 'Why do you lament the transitoriness of living things? How could I exist if all those of my species which came before me had not died?'

However much the plays and the masks on the world's stage may change it is always the same actors who appear. We sit together and talk and grow excited, and our eyes glitter and our voices grow shriller: just so did *others* sit and talk a thousand years ago: it was the same thing, and it was the *same people*: and it will be just so a thousand years hence. The contrivance which prevents us from perceiving this is *time*.

One would do well to make a clear distinction between *metempsychosis*, which is the transference of the entire so-called soul into another body, and *palingenesis*, which is the *decomposition* and reconstruction of the individual in which *will* alone persists and, assuming the shape of a new being, receives a new intellect.

Throughout all time it is the male sex which stores up the will of the human species and the female which stores up the intellect. Thus each of us has a paternal and a maternal constituent; and as these are united through procreation, so they are sundered again through death, which is thus the end of the individual. It is this individual whose death we grieve so much for, in the feeling that it is really lost to us, that it was no more than a compound which has now been irretrievably broken up. Yet in all this we must not forget that the hereditariness of intellect from the mother is not so firm and unconditional as that of will from the father, the reason being the secondary and merely physical nature of intellect and its total dependence on the organism.

One can thus regard every human being from two opposed viewpoints. From the one he is the fleeting individual, burdened with error and sorrow and with a beginning and an end in time; from the other he is the indestructible primal being which is objectified in everything that exists.

8

Thrasymachus To sum up, what shall I be after my death? Be clear and precise!

    Philalethes Everything and nothing.

Thrasymachus As I expected! For the solution to a problem
– a contradiction. That trick is very worn-out.

Philalethes To answer transcendent questions in language
made for immanent knowledge is bound to lead to contradic-
tions.

Thrasymachus What do you call transcendent and what
immanent knowledge? – I too am familiar with these expressions; I learned them from my professor, but only as predicates
of the good Lord God, with whom his philosophy was exclusively preoccupied, as was quite right and proper. If God is
somewhere in the world he is immanent; but if he sits somewhere outside it, he is transcendent. – Well, that is clear, that's
something you can get hold of! You know where you are with
that. But no one can any longer understand your old-fashioned
Kantian jargon. What is it supposed to mean?

Philalethes Transcendent knowledge is that which, passing
beyond all possible experience, strives to determine the nature of
things as they are in themselves; immanent knowledge, on the
other hand, is that which confines itself within the bounds of
possible experience and can therefore speak only of phenomena.
– You, as an individual, will come to an end with your death.
But your individuality is not your essential and ultimate being,
only a manifestation of it: your individuality is not the thing in
itself but only the phenomenal form of it which appears under
the aspect of time and consequently has a beginning and an
end. Your being in itself, on the other hand, knows neither
time nor beginning nor end, nor the bounds of a given individuality; thus no individuality can exclude it – it exists in everyone
everywhere. In the former sense, therefore, you will when you
die become nothing, in the latter everything. That is why I said
that after your death you will be everything and nothing. Your
question hardly permits of a better short answer than this, even
though it does contain a contradiction; and it does so precisely
because your life is in time but your immortality is in eternity. –
Thus your immortality can also be termed an indestructibility
without continued existence – which again amounts to a contradiction.

Thrasymachus Well, I wouldn't give twopence for your immortality if it doesn't include the continued existence of my individuality.

Philalethes But perhaps you would be willing to bargain a little. Suppose I guarantee you the continued existence of your individuality, but on condition it is preceded by a completely unconscious death-sleep of three months.

Thrasymachus I would agree to that.

Philalethes But since when we are completely unconscious we have no notion of the passage of time, it is all one to us whether, while we are lying in that death-sleep, three months or ten thousand years pass in the conscious world. For in either case, when we awake we have to take on trust how long we have been sleeping. So that it will be all the same to you whether your individuality is restored to you after three months or ten thousand years.

Thrasymachus That cannot very well be denied.

Philalethes But now, if after these ten thousand years have passed it was forgotten to wake you up, this would not, I think, be a very great misfortune, since your period of non-being would have been so long compared with your brief period of being you would have got quite used to it. What is certain, however, is that you would not have the least idea you had failed to be woken up. And you would be completely content with the whole thing if you knew that the mysterious mechanism which moves your present phenomenal form had not ceased for one moment throughout those ten thousand years to produce and move other phenomena of the same sort.

Thrasymachus No, you can't cheat me out of my individuality in that way. I have stipulated that my individuality should continue to exist, and I cannot be reconciled to its loss by mechanisms and phenomena. I, I, I want to exist! *that* is what I want, and not an existence I first have to be argued into believing I possess.

Philalethes But just look around you! That which cries 'I, I, I want to exist' is not you alone; it is everything, absolutely everything that has the slightest trace of consciousness. So that this desire in you is precisely that which is *not* individual but common to everything without exception: it arises not from the individuality but from *existence* as such, is intrinsic to everything that *exists* and indeed the reason *why* it exists, and it is consequently satisfied by existence *as such*: it is this alone to which this desire applies, and not exclusively to some particular individual existence. That which desires existence so impetuously is only *indirectly* the individual! directly and intrinsically it is will to live as such, which is one and the same in all things. Since, then, existence itself is the free work, indeed the mere reflection of the will, the will cannot be deprived of it: the will is, however, temporarily satisfied by it, in so far, that is, as what is eternally unsatisfied can be satisfied at all. Individualities are a matter of indifference to the will; it is not concerned with them, although it seems to be so, because the individual has no direct knowledge of it except in himself. The effect of this is to make the individual expend more care on preserving his existence than he otherwise would, and thereby ensure the preservation of his species. From this it follows that individuality is not a form of perfection but a limitation: thus to be free of it is not a loss but rather a gain. So cease worrying about it: truly, if you knew your own being to its very depths as the universal will to live which you are – such worries would then seem to you childish and altogether ludicrous.

Thrasymachus Childish and altogether ludicrous is what you yourself are, and all philosophers; and if a grown-up man like me spends fifteen minutes with fools of this kind it is merely a way of passing the time. I've now got more important things to do. Good-bye!

ON SUICIDE

I

As far as I can see, it is only the monotheistic, that is to say Jewish, religions whose members regard self-destruction as a crime. This is all the more striking in that neither in the Old nor in the New Testament is there to be found any prohibition or even definite disapproval of it; so that religious teachers have to base their proscription of suicide on philosophical grounds of their own invention, which are however so poor that what their arguments lack in strength they have to try to make up for by the strength of the terms in which they express their abhorrence; that is to say, they resort to abuse. Thus we hear that suicide is the most cowardly of acts, that only a madman would commit it, and similar insipidities; or the senseless assertion that suicide is 'wrong', though it is obvious there is nothing in the world a man has a more incontestable *right* to than his own life and person. Let us for once allow moral feelings to decide this question, and compare the impression made on us by the news that an acquaintance of ours has committed a crime, for instance a murder, an act of cruelty, a betrayal, a theft, with that produced by the news that he has voluntarily ended his life. While the former will evoke a lively indignation, anger, the demand for punishment or revenge, the latter will excite pity and sorrow, which are more likely to be accompanied by admiration for his courage than by moral disapproval. Who has not had acquaintances, friends, relatives who have departed this world voluntarily? – and is one supposed to think of them with repugnance, as if they were criminals? In my opinion it ought rather to be demanded of the clergy that they tell us by what authority they go to their pulpits or their desks and brand as a *crime* an action which many people we honour and love have performed and deny an honourable burial to those who

77

have departed this world voluntarily – since they cannot point to a single biblical authority, nor produce a single sound philosophical argument; it being made clear that what one wants are *reasons* and not empty phrases or abuse. If the criminal law proscribes suicide this is no valid reason for the Church to do so, and is moreover a decidedly ludicrous proceeding, for what punishment can deter him who is looking for death? If one punishes attempted suicide, it is the ineptitude of the attempt one punishes.

The only cogent moral argument against suicide is that it is opposed to the achievement of the highest moral goal, inasmuch as it substitutes for a true redemption from this world of misery a merely apparent one. But it is a very long way from a mistake of this kind to a crime, which is what the Christian clergy want to call it.

Christianity carries in its innermost heart the truth that suffering (the Cross) is the true aim of life: that is why it repudiates suicide, which is opposed to this aim, while antiquity from a lower viewpoint approved of and indeed honoured it. This argument against suicide is however an ascetic one, and is therefore valid only from a far higher ethical standpoint than any which European moral philosophers have ever assumed. If we descend from this very high standpoint there no longer remains any tenable moral reason for damning suicide. It therefore seems that the extraordinary zeal in opposing it displayed by the clergy of monotheistic religions – a zeal which is not supported by the Bible or by any cogent reasons – must have some hidden reason behind it: may this not be that the voluntary surrender of life is an ill compliment to him who said that all things were very good? If so, it is another instance of the obligatory optimism of these religions, which denounces self-destruction so as not to be denounced by it.

2

It will generally be found that where the terrors of life come to outweigh the terrors of death a man will put an end to his life.

But the terrors of death offer considerable resistance: they stand like a sentinel at the exit gate. Perhaps there is no one alive who would not already have put an end to his life if this end were something purely negative, a sudden cessation of existence. But there is something positive in it as well: the destruction of the body. This is a deterrent, because the body is the phenomenal form of the will to live.

The struggle with that sentinel is as a rule, however, not as hard as it may seem to us from a distance: the reason is the antagonism between spiritual and physical suffering. For when we are in great or chronic physical pain we are indifferent to all other troubles: all we are concerned about is recovering. In the same way, great spiritual suffering makes us insensible to physical pain: we despise it: indeed, if it should come to outweigh the other it becomes a beneficial distraction, an interval in spiritual suffering. It is this which makes suicide easier: for the physical pain associated with it loses all significance in the eyes of one afflicted by excessive spiritual suffering.

ON WOMEN

1

SCHILLER's whole comprehensive poem *Würde der Frauen*, with its effects of antithesis and contrast, fails, in my opinion, to express what is truly to be praised in women as well as do these few words of Jouy: *Sans les femmes, le commencement de notre vie serait privé de secours, le milieu de plaisirs, et la fin de consolation.*[1] Byron says the same thing with more pathos in *Sardanapolis.*[2]

> The very first
> Of human life must spring from woman's breast,
> Your first small words are taught you from her lips,
> Your first tears quench'd by her, and your last sighs
> Too often breathed out in a woman's hearing,
> When men have shrunk from the ignoble care
> Of watching the last hour of him who led them.

Both indicate the correct viewpoint for estimating the value of women.

2

One needs only to see the way she is built to realize that woman is not intended for great mental or for great physical labour. She expiates the guilt of life not through activity but through suffering, through the pains of childbirth, caring for the child and subjection to the man, to whom she should be a

---

1. Johann Christoph Friedrich von Schiller (1759–1805) is traditionally Germany's second greatest poet, but much of his verse, of which *The Dignity* (or Merit or Worth) *of Women* is a once-famous example, is of the 'good bad' variety, like Walter Scott's. His true genius lay in the field of popular drama, and his best plays are still much performed. Victor Jouy (1764–1846), dramatist.

2. Act I, scene 2.

patient and cheering companion. Great suffering, joy, exertion, is not for her: her life should flow by more quietly, trivially, gently than the man's without being essentially happier or unhappier.

3

Women are suited to being the nurses and teachers of our earliest childhood precisely because they themselves are childish, silly and short-sighted, in a word big children, their whole lives long: a kind of intermediate stage between the child and the man, who is the actual human being, 'man'. One has only to watch a girl playing with a child, dancing and singing with it the whole day, and then ask oneself what, with the best will in the world, a man could do in her place.

4

In the girl nature has had in view what could in theatrical terms be called a stage-effect: it has provided her with super-abundant beauty and charm for a few years at the expense of the whole remainder of her life, so that during these years she may so capture the imagination of a man that he is carried away into undertaking to support her honourably in some form or another for the rest of her life, a step he would seem hardly likely to take for purely rational considerations. Thus nature has equipped women, as it has all its creatures, with the tools and weapons she needs for securing her existence, and at just the time she needs them; in doing which nature has acted with its usual economy. For just as the female ant loses its wings after mating, since they are then superfluous, indeed harmful to the business of raising the family, so the woman usually loses her beauty after one or two childbeds, and probably for the same reason.

5

The nobler and more perfect a thing is, the later and more slowly does it mature. The man attains the maturity of his reasoning powers and spiritual faculties hardly before his twenty-eighth year; the woman with her eighteenth. And even then it is only reasoning power of a sort: a very limited sort. Thus women remain children all their lives, never see anything but what is closest to them, cleave to the present moment, take appearance for reality and prefer trifles to the most important affairs. For reason is the faculty by virtue of which man lives not merely in the present, as the animal does, but surveys and ponders past and future, from which arises his capacity for foresight, his care and trouble, and the anxiety he so frequently feels. As a consequence of her weaker reasoning powers, woman has a smaller share of the advantages and disadvantages these bring with them: she is, rather, a mental myopic, in that her intuitive understanding sees very clearly what is close to her but has a very narrow field of vision from which what is distant is excluded; so that what is absent, past or to come makes a very much weaker impression on women than it does on us, which is the origin of their much greater tendency to squandering, a tendency which sometimes verges on madness. Women think in their hearts that the man's business is to make money and theirs is to spend it: where possible during the man's lifetime, but in any case after his death. That the man hands over to them for housekeeping the money he has earned strengthens them in this belief. – Whatever disadvantages all this may bring with it, it has this good effect, that woman is more absorbed in the present than we are, so that, if the present is endurable at all, she enjoys it more, and this produces that cheerfulness characteristic of her through which she is so suited to entertain and, if need be, console the care-laden man.

To consult women when you are in difficulties, as the ancient Teutons did, is by no means a bad idea: for their way of looking at things is quite different from ours, especially in their propensity for keeping in view the shortest road to a desired goal and in general what lies closest to hand, which we usually overlook precisely because it is right in front of our noses. In addition, women are decidedly more prosaic than we are and see no more in things than is really there, while we, if our passions are aroused, will easily exaggerate and indulge in imaginings.

It is for this reason too that women display more pity, and consequently more philanthropy and sympathy with the unfortunate, than men do; on the other hand, they are inferior to men in respect of justice, honesty and conscientiousness: for as a result of their weaker reasoning power women are as a rule far more affected by what is present, visible and immediately real than they are by abstract ideas, standing maxims, previous decisions or in general by regard for what is far off, in the past or still to come. Thus, while they possess the first and chief virtue, they are deficient in the secondary one which is often necessary for achieving the first. – One must accordingly say that the fundamental defect of the female character is *a lack of a sense of justice*. This originates first and foremost in their want of rationality and capacity for reflexion but it is strengthened by the fact that, as the weaker sex, they are driven to rely not on force but on cunning: hence their instinctive subtlety and their ineradicable tendency to tell lies: for, as nature has equipped the lion with claws and teeth, the elephant with tusks, the wild boar with fangs, the bull with horns and the cuttlefish with ink, so it has equipped woman with the power of dissimulation as her means of attack and defence, and has transformed into this gift all the strength it has bestowed on man in the form of physical strength and the power of reasoning. Dissimulation is thus inborn in her and consequently to be found in the stupid woman almost as often as in the clever one. To make use of it at every opportunity is as natural to her as it is for an animal to employ its means of defence whenever it is attacked, and when she does so she feels that to some extent she is only exercising her rights. A completely truthful woman who does not practise dissimulation is perhaps an impossibility, which is why women see through the dissimulation of others so easily it is inadvisable to attempt it with them. – But this fundamental defect which I have said they possess, together with all that is associated with it, gives rise to falsity, unfaithfulness, treachery, ingratitude, etc. Women are guilty of perjury far more often than men. It is questionable whether they ought to be allowed to take an oath at all.

6

To take care of the propagation of the human race nature has chosen the young, strong and handsome men, so that the race shall not degenerate. This is the firm will of nature in this matter, and its expression is the passion of women. In antiquity and force this law precedes every other: so woe to him who sets his rights and interests in the path of this law: whatever he says or does they will, at the first serious encounter, be mercilessly crushed. For the secret, unspoken, indeed unconscious, but nonetheless inborn morality of women is: 'We are justified in deceiving those who, because they provide a meagre support for us, the individual, think they have acquired a right over the species. The character and consequently the well-being of the species has, through the next generation proceeding from us, been placed in our hands and entrusted to our care: let us discharge that trust conscientiously.' Women are, however, by no means conscious of this supreme law *in abstracto*, only *in concreto*; and they have no way of giving expression to it apart from their mode of action if the occasion presents itself; and then they are usually less troubled by their conscience than we suppose, because they are aware in the darkest recesses of their heart that in violating their duty to the individual they are all the better fulfilling their duty to the species, whose rights are incomparably greater.

Because fundamentally women exist solely for the propagation of the race and find in this their entire vocation, they are altogether more involved with the species than with individuals, and in their hearts take the affairs of the species more seriously than they do those of the individual. This gives their entire nature and all their activities a certain levity and in general a direction fundamentally different from those of the man: which is why dissention between married couples is so frequent and indeed almost the normal case.

7

Men are by nature merely indifferent to one another; but women are by nature enemies. The reason is no doubt that that *odium figulinum* [3] which with men does not go beyond the bounds of the particular guild, with women embraces the whole sex, because they are all engaged in the same trade. Even when they simply pass in the street they look at one another like Guelphs and Ghibellines; and when two women meet for the first time there is clearly more constraint and pretence involved than in the case of two men: so that when two women exchange compliments it sounds much more ludicrous than when two men do so. Further, while a man will as a rule still preserve some degree of consideration and humanity even when addressing men very much his inferior, it is intolerable to see with what haughty disdain an aristocratic woman usually speaks to women who are beneath her (I am not referring to servants). The reason for this may be that with women all differences in rank are far more precarious than they are with us, and can be altered or abolished much more quickly, because in our case a hundred different considerations are involved, while in theirs only one is decisive, namely which man they have succeeded in attracting. Another reason may be that, because they are all in the same profession, they all stand much closer to one another than men do, and consequently strive to emphasize differences in rank.

8

Only a male intellect clouded by the sexual drive could call the stunted, narrow-shouldered, broad-hipped and short-legged sex the fair sex: for it is with this drive that all its beauty is bound up. More fittingly than the fair sex, women could be called the *unaesthetic* sex. Neither for music, nor poetry, nor the plastic arts do they possess any real feeling or receptivity: if they affect to do so, it is merely mimicry in service of their effort to please. This comes from the fact that they are incapable of taking a

3. Mutual dislike of those in the same trade.

purely objective interest in anything whatever, and the reason
for this is, I think, as follows. Man strives in everything for a
direct domination over things, either by comprehending or by
subduing them. But woman is everywhere and always relegated
to a merely *indirect* domination, which is achieved by means of
man, who is consequently the only thing she has to dominate
directly. Thus it lies in the nature of women to regard everything simply as a means of capturing a man, and their interest
in anything else is only simulated, is no more than a detour, i.e.
amounts to coquetry and mimicry. One has only to observe how
they behave in the theatre or at operas and concerts, e.g. the
childish unconcern with which they go on chattering away
during the most beautiful parts of the greatest masterpieces. If
it is true the Greeks refused to allow women into the theatre,
they did the right thing: at least one would have been able to
hear what was going on. – Nor can one expect anything else
from women if one considers that the most eminent heads of
the entire sex have proved incapable of a single truly great,
genuine and original achievement in art, or indeed of creating
anything at all of lasting value: this strikes one most forcibly
in regard to painting, since they are just as capable of mastering
its technique as we are, and indeed paint very busily, yet cannot
point to a single great painting; the reason being precisely that
they lack all objectivity of mind, which is what painting
demands above all else. Isolated and partial exceptions do not
alter the case: women, taken as a whole, are and remain thorough
and incurable philistines: so that, with the extremely absurd
arrangement by which they share the rank and title of their
husband, they are a continual spur to his *ignoble* ambitions.
They are *sexus sequior*, the inferior second sex in *every* respect:
one should be indulgent towards their weaknesses, but to pay
them honour is ridiculous beyond measure and demeans us
even in their eyes. – This is how the peoples of antiquity and of
the Orient have regarded women; they have recognized what is
the proper position for women far better than we have, we with
our Old French gallantry and insipid women-veneration, that
highest flower of Christian-Germanic stupidity which has

served only to make women so rude and arrogant that one is sometimes reminded of the sacred apes of Benares which, conscious of their own sanctity and inviolability, thought themselves at liberty to do whatever they pleased.

Woman in the Occident, that is to say the 'lady', finds herself in a false position: for woman is by no means fitted to be the object of our veneration, to hold her head higher than the man or to enjoy equal rights with him. The consequences of this false position are sufficiently obvious. It would thus be a very desirable thing if this number two of the human race were again put in her natural place in Europe too, and a limit set to the unnaturalness called a lady at which all Asia laughs and which Greece and Rome would laugh at too if they could see it: the consequences for the social, civil and political life of Europe would be incalculably beneficial. The European lady is a creature which ought not to exist at all: what there ought to be is housewives and girls who hope to become housewives and who are therefore educated, not in arrogant haughtiness, but in domesticity and submissiveness. It is precisely because there are *ladies* that European women of a lower status, which is to say the great majority of the sex, are much more unhappy than they are in the Orient.

9

In our monogamous part of the world, to marry means to halve one's rights and double one's duties. But when the law conceded women equal rights with men it should at the same time have endowed them with masculine reasoning powers. What is actually the case is that the more those rights and privileges the law accords to women exceed those which are natural to them, the more it reduces the number of women who actually participate in these benefits; and then the remainder are deprived of their natural rights by just the amount these few receive in excess of theirs: for, because of the unnaturally privileged position enjoyed by women as a consequence of monogamy and the marriage laws accompanying it, which regard women as entirely equal to men (which they are in no respect), prudent and cautious men very often hesitate before making so great a sacrifice as is involved in entering into so inequitable a contract; so that while among polygamous peoples every woman gets taken care of, among the monogamous the number of married women is limited and there remains over a quantity of unsupported women who, in the upper classes, vegetate on as useless old maids, and in the lower are obliged to undertake laborious work they are constitutionally unfitted for or become *filles de joie,* whose lives are as devoid of *joie* as they are of honour but who, given the prevailing circumstances, are necessary for the gratification of the male sex and therefore come to constitute a recognized class, with the specific task of preserving the virtue of those women more favoured by fate who have found a man to support them or may reasonably hope to find one. There are 80,000 prostitutes in London alone: and what are they if not sacrifices on the altar of monogamy? These poor women are the inevitable counterpart and natural complement to the European lady, with all her arrogance and pretension. For the female sex viewed *as a whole* polygamy is therefore a real benefit; on the other hand there appears no rational ground why a man whose wife suffers from a chronic illness, or has remained unfruitful, or has gradually grown too old for him, should not take a second.

There can be no argument about polygamy: it is a fact to be met with everywhere, and the only question is how to *regulate* it. For who is really a monogamist? We all live in polygamy, *at least* for a time and usually for good. Since every man needs many women, there could be nothing more just than that he should be free, indeed obliged, to support many women. This would also mean the restoration of woman to her rightful and natural position, the subordinate one, and the abolition from the world of the *lady*, with her ridiculous claims to respect and veneration; there would then be only *women*, and no longer *unhappy women*, of which Europe is at present full.

ON THINKING FOR YOURSELF

1

As the biggest library if it is in disorder is not as useful as a small but well-arranged one, so you may accumulate a vast amount of knowledge but it will be of far less value to you than a much smaller amount if you have not thought it over for yourself; because only through ordering what you know by comparing every truth with every other truth can you take complete possession of your knowledge and get it into your power. You can think about only what you know, so you ought to learn something; on the other hand, you can know only what you have thought about.

Now you can apply yourself voluntarily to reading and learning, but you cannot really apply yourself to thinking: thinking has to be kindled, as a fire is by a draught, and kept going by some kind of interest in its object, which may be an objective interest or merely a subjective one. The latter is possible only with things that affect us personally, the former only to those heads who think by nature, to whom thinking is as natural as breathing, and these are very rare. That is why most scholars do so little of it.

2

The difference between the effect produced on the mind by thinking for yourself and that produced by reading is incredibly great, so that the original difference which made one head decide for thinking and another for reading is continually increased. For reading forcibly imposes on the mind thoughts that are as foreign to its mood and direction at the moment of reading as the signet is to the wax upon which it impresses its seal. The mind is totally subjected to an external compulsion to think this or that for which it has no inclination and is not in the mood. On the other hand, when it is thinking for itself it is following its own inclination, as this has been more closely determined either by its immediate surroundings or by some recollection or other: for its visible surroundings do not impose some *single* thought on the mind, as reading does; they merely provide it with occasion and matter for thinking the thoughts appropriate to its nature and present mood. The result is that *much* reading robs the mind of all elasticity, as the continual pressure of a weight does a spring, and that the surest way of never having any thoughts of your own is to pick up a book every time you have a free moment. The practice of doing this is the reason erudition makes most men duller and sillier than they are by nature and robs their writings of all effectiveness: they are in Pope's words:

> For ever reading, never to be read.

3

Fundamentally it is only our own basic thoughts that possess truth and life, for only these do we really understand through and through. The thoughts of another that we have read are crumbs from another's table, the cast-off clothes of an unfamiliar guest.

4

Reading is merely a surrogate for thinking for yourself; it means letting someone else direct your thoughts. Many books, moreover, serve merely to show how many ways there are of being wrong, and how far astray you yourself would go if you followed their guidance. – You should read only when your own thoughts dry up, which will of course happen frequently enough even to the best heads; but to banish your own thoughts so as to take up a book is a sin against the Holy Ghost; it is like deserting untrammelled nature to look at a herbarium or engravings of landscapes.

It may sometimes happen that a truth, an insight, which you

have slowly and laboriously puzzled out by thinking for yourself could easily have been found already written in a book; but it is a hundred times more valuable if you have arrived at it by thinking for yourself. For only then will it enter your thought-system as an integral part and living member, be perfectly and firmly consistent with it and in accord with all its other consequences and conclusions, bear the hue, colour and stamp of your whole manner of thinking, and have arrived at just the moment it was needed; thus it will stay firmly and for ever lodged in your mind. This is a perfect application, indeed explanation, of Goethe's lines:

> Was du ererbt von deinen Vätern hast,
> Erwirb es, um es zu besitzen.[1]

For the man who thinks for himself becomes acquainted with the authorities for his opinions only after he has acquired them and merely as a confirmation of them, while the book-philosopher starts with his authorities, in that he constructs his opinions by collecting together the opinions of others: his mind then compares with that of the former as an automaton compares with a living man.

A truth that has merely been learnt adheres to us only as an artificial limb, a false tooth, a wax nose does, or at most like transplanted skin; but a truth won by thinking for ourself is like a natural limb: it alone really belongs to us. This is what determines the difference between a thinker and a mere scholar.

5

People who pass their lives in reading and acquire their wisdom from books are like those who learn about a country from travel descriptions: they can impart information about a great number of things, but at bottom they possess no connected, clear, thorough knowledge of what the country is like. On the other hand, people who pass their lives in thinking are like those who

1. What you have inherited from your forefathers you must first win for yourself if you are to possess it.

have visited the country themselves: they alone are really familiar with it, possess connected knowledge of it and are truly at home in it.

6

A man who thinks for himself is related to the ordinary book-philosopher as an eyewitness is to an historian: the former speaks from his own immediate experience. That is why all men who think for themselves are in fundamental agreement: their differences spring only from their differing standpoints; for they merely express what they have objectively apprehended. The book-philosopher, on the contrary, reports what this man has said and that has thought and the other has objected, etc. Then he compares, weighs, criticizes these statements, and thus tries to get to the truth of the matter, in which respect he exactly resembles the critical historian.

7

Mere experience is no more a substitute for thinking than reading is. Pure empiricism is related to thinking as eating is to digestion and assimilation. When empiricism boasts that it alone has, through its discoveries, advanced human knowledge, it is as if the mouth should boast that it alone keeps the body alive.

8

The characteristic mark of minds of the first rank is the immediacy of all their judgements. Everything they produce is the result of thinking for themselves and already in the way it is spoken everywhere announces itself as such. He who truly thinks for himself is like a monarch, in that he recognizes no one over him. His judgements, like the decisions of a monarch, arise directly from his own absolute power. He no more accepts authorities than a monarch does orders, and he acknowledges the validity of nothing he has not himself confirmed.

9

In the realm of actuality, however fair, happy and pleasant we may find it, we are nonetheless always under the influence of gravity, which we have continually to overcome: in the realm of thought, on the contrary, we are disembodied minds, weightless and without needs or cares. That is why there is no happiness on earth to compare with that which a beautiful and fruitful mind finds in a propitious hour in itself.

10

There are very many thoughts which have value for him who thinks them, but only a few of them possess the power of engaging the interest of a reader after they have been written down.

11

Yet, all the same, only that possesses true value which you have thought in the first instance *for your own instruction*. Thinkers can be divided into those who think in the first instance for their own instruction and those who do so for the instruction of others. The former are genuine *thinkers for themselves* in both senses of the words: they are the true *philosophers*. They alone are in earnest. The pleasure and happiness of their existence consists in thinking. The latter are *sophists*: they want to *appear* as thinkers and seek their happiness in what they hope thereby to get from others. This is what they are in earnest about. To which of these two classes a man belongs may quickly be seen by his whole style and manner. Lichtenberg is an example of the former class, Herder certainly belongs to the latter.[2]

2. Georg Christoph Lichtenberg (1742–99), aphorist and satirist. Johann Gottfried von Herder (1744–1803), theologian, philosopher and man of letters.

When you consider how great and how immediate is the *problem of existence*, this ambiguous, tormented, fleeting, dreamlike existence – so great and so immediate that as soon as you are aware of it it overshadows and obscures all other problems and aims; and when you then see how men, with a few rare exceptions, have no clear awareness of this problem, indeed seem not to be conscious of it at all, but concern themselves with anything rather than with this problem and live on taking thought only for the day and for the hardly longer span of their own individual future, either expressly refusing to consider this problem or contenting themselves with some system of popular metaphysics; when, I say, you consider this, you may come to the opinion that man can be called a *thinking being* only in a very broad sense of that term and no longer feel very much surprise at any thoughtlessness or silliness whatever, but will realize, rather, that while the intellectual horizon of the normal man is wider than that of the animal – whose whole existence is, as it were, one continual present, with no consciousness of past or future – it is not so immeasurably wider as is generally supposed.

ON RELIGION: A DIALOGUE

Demopheles Between ourselves, my dear friend, I don't much like the way you have of displaying your talent for philosophy by making sarcastic remarks about religion or even openly ridiculing it. Every man's faith is sacred to him, therefore it ought to be sacred to you too.

Philalethes Nego consequentiam![1] I can't see why, because other people are simple-minded, I should respect a pack of lies. What I respect is truth, therefore I can't respect what opposes truth. Just as the jurist's motto is: *fiat justitia et pereat mundus,* so my motto is: *vigeat veritas et pereat mundus.* Every profession ought to have an analogous device.

Demopheles Then I suppose the physician's would be: *fiant pilulae et pereat mundus* – which would be the one most likely to be realized.[2]

Philalethes Heaven forfend! You must take everything *cum grano salis.*[3]

Demopheles Very well: but that applies to you too: you've got to take religion *cum grano salis*: you've got to see that the needs of ordinary people have to be met in a way they can understand. Religion is the only means of introducing some notion of the high significance of life into the uncultivated heads of the masses, deep sunk as they are in mean pursuits and material drudgery, and of making it palpable to them. Man, taken by and large, has by nature no mind for anything but the satisfaction of his physical needs and desires, and when these are satisfied for a little entertainment and recreation. Philosophers and founders of religions come into the world to shake him out of his stupe-

1. I deny your conclusion!
2. Let justice be done though the world perish. Let truth prosper though the world perish. Let pills be distributed though the world perish.
3. With a pinch of salt.

95

faction and to point to the lofty meaning of existence: philosophers for the few, the emancipated, founders of religions for
the many, for mankind as a whole. Philosophy isn't for everyone – as your friend Plato said and as you shouldn't forget.
Religion is the metaphysics of the people, which they absolutely
must be allowed to keep: and that means you have to show an
outward respect for it, since to discredit it is to take it away
from them. Just as there is folk-poetry and, in the proverbs,
folk-wisdom, so there has to be folk-metaphysics: for men have
an absolute need for an *interpretation of life*, and it has to be one
they are capable of understanding. That is why it is always
clothed in allegory; and, as far as its practical effect as a guide
to behaviour and its effect on morale as a means of consolation
and comfort in suffering and death are concerned, it does as
much perhaps as truth itself would do if we possessed it. Don't
worry yourself about the baroque and apparently paradoxical
forms it assumes: for you, with your learning and culture,
have no idea how tortuous and roundabout a route is required
to take profound truths to the mass of the people, with their
lack of them. The people have no direct access to truth; the
various religions are simply schemata by which they grasp it and
picture it, but with which it is inseparably linked. Therefore,
my dear chap, I hope you'll forgive me for saying that to ridicule
them is to be both narrow-minded and unjust.

Philalethes But isn't it just as narrow-minded and unjust to
demand that there should exist no other metaphysics except this
one cut to the requirements of the people's wants and capacities?
that its teachings and doctrine should mark the limit of inquiry
and be the guide and model for all thinking, so that the metaphysics of the few and emancipated, as you call them, must
amount to nothing but a confirmation, fortification and illumination of your metaphysics of the people? that the highest powers
of the human mind should thus lie unused and undeveloped,
should indeed be nipped in the bud, in case their activities might
happen to run counter to your folk-metaphysics? And do the
pretensions of religion amount at bottom to anything less than
this? Is it proper and becoming in that which is intolerance and

pitilessness itself to preach tolerance and pity? I call on heretic courts and inquisitions, religious wars and crusades, Socrates' poison cup and Bruno's and Vanini's blazing pyres to bear witness![4] And even if, as I grant, that kind of thing doesn't go on nowadays, what could stand more in the way of genuine philosophy, of honest inquiry after truth, which is the noblest calling of noblest men, than that conventional metaphysics to which the state has granted a monopoly and whose propositions are hammered into everyone's head in his childhood so earnestly and so deeply and firmly that, unless it is of a miraculous degree of elasticity, it retains their impress for ever, so that his capacity for thinking for himself and for making unprejudiced judgements – a capacity which is in any case far from strong – is once and for all paralysed and ruined?

Demopheles What all this really means is that people have acquired a conviction they aren't willing to give up in exchange for yours.

Philalethes If only it *were* a conviction, and one founded on reason! Then it could be combatted with reasons, and we should be fighting on equal terms. But it is common knowledge that religions don't want conviction, on the basis of reasons, but faith, on the basis of revelation. And the capacity for faith is at its strongest in childhood: which is why religions apply themselves before all else to getting these tender years into their possession. It is in this way, even more than by threats and stories of miracles, that the doctrines of faith strike roots: for if, in earliest childhood, a man has certain principles and doctrines repeatedly recited to him with abnormal solemnity and with an air of supreme earnestness such as he has never before beheld, and at the same time the possibility of doubt is never so much as touched on, or if it is only in order to describe it as the first step towards eternal perdition, then the impression produced will be so profound that in almost every case the man will be almost as incapable of doubting this doctrine as of doubting his own existence, so that hardly one in a thousand will then possess

---

4. Giordano Bruno (1548–1600), burned alive for heresy. Lucilio Vanini (1585–1619), burned alive for 'atheism and blasphemy'.

the firmness of mind seriously and honestly to ask himself: is this true? The expression *esprits forts*, strong minds, applied to those who do still possess it, is more fitting than those who use it know. But for the remainder, however, there is nothing so absurd or revolting that they will not firmly believe it once they have been inoculated with it in this fashion. If, for example, the killing of a heretic or an unbeliever were declared to be an essential condition for salvation, then almost every one of them would make doing so one of the main objectives of his life and in death the memory of the deed would provide consolation and strength; as, indeed, almost every Spaniard in fact used to consider an *auto da fé* a most pious and God-pleasing act; to which we have a counterpart in India in the religious fellowship of the Thugs which the English suppressed only quite recently by numerous executions: its members gave proof of their religiousness and of their worship of their goddess Kali by treacherously murdering their friends and travelling companions whenever the occasion offered and making away with their possessions, under the firm illusion that they were doing something praiseworthy and promoting their eternal salvation. The power of religious dogmas imprinted in early years is such that they are capable of stifling conscience and finally all pity and humanity. If you want to see with your own eyes and from close to what early inoculation with faith can do, look at the English. Nature has favoured them before all other nations and furnished them with more understanding, mind, judgement and firmness of character than all the rest; yet they have been degraded lower than all the rest, indeed been rendered almost contemptible, by their stupid church superstition, which infiltrates all their capabilities like an *idée fixe,* a downright monomania. The only reason for this is that education is in the hands of the clergy, who take care so to imprint all the articles of faith in earliest youth that it produces a kind of partial paralysis of the brain, which then gives rise to that lifelong imbecile bigotry through which even people otherwise in the highest degree intelligent degrade themselves and make a quite misleading impression on the rest of the world. But when we consider how essential it is to a masterly performance of this sort that the inoculation with faith should take place during the tenderest years, then the sending of missionaries will no longer seem to us merely the height of importunity, arrogance and impertinence, it will also seem absurd when it is not limited to peoples still in the state of childhood, such as Hottentots, Kaffirs, South Sea Islanders and the like, among whom it has met with the success one would expect; while in India, on the contrary, the Brahmins meet the sermons of missionaries with condescending smiles or a shrug of the shoulders, and among this people in general all attempts at conversion have, the most comfortable opportunity for it notwithstanding, met with utter failure. For, as I have said, childhood and not adulthood is the time to sow the seed of faith, especially when by the time adulthood is reached an earlier seed has already taken root; acquired *conviction*, however, to which adult converts pretend, is as a rule only a mask for some personal interest or other. It is precisely because people feel that this must almost always be the case that a man who changes his religion after reaching years of discretion is everywhere despised by the majority: and this contempt likewise reveals that they regard religion, not as a matter of reasoned conviction, but one of faith inoculated early in life and before having been subjected to any sort of test. That they are justified in their opinion appears from the fact that it is not merely the blindly believing crowd which remains faithful to the religion of its respective fatherland – the priesthood of every religion, which has studied the sources and grounds and dogmas and controversies of this religion, does so too; so that for a priest to cross over from one religion or confession to another is the rarest thing in the world. Thus we see, for example, the Catholic clergy totally convinced of the truth of all the doctrines of its Church, and the Protestant clergy likewise convinced of the truth of all the doctrines of *its* Church, and both defending the doctrines of their confession with equal zeal. Yet this conviction depends entirely on the country in which each was born: to the South German priest the truth of the Catholic dogma is perfectly apparent, but to the North German priest it is that of

Protestant dogma which is perfectly apparent. If, then, these convictions, and others like them, rest on objective grounds, these grounds must be climatic; such convictions must be like flowers, the one flourishing only here, the other only there. But the convictions of those who are thus locally convinced are taken on trust everywhere.

Demopheles That does no harm and makes no essential difference; and Protestantism is in fact more suited to the North, Catholicism to the South.

Philalethes It would seem so. But I have adopted a higher viewpoint and I keep a more important objective in sight: advancement of the knowledge of truth in the human race. So far as this is concerned, it is a terrible thing that everyone, wherever he may be born, should have certain assertions impressed on him in earliest youth, together with the assurance that to call them in doubt is to imperil his eternal salvation. I call this a terrible thing because these assertions are largely concerned with what is the basis of all other knowledge we possess, so that a certain point of view in respect to all knowledge is fixed once and for all and, if these assertions should be untrue, it is a permanently perverse point of view; and since, further, their consequences and conclusions extend over our entire system of knowledge, the totality of human understanding is falsified through and through by them. All literature provides evidence of this, that of the Middle Ages most strikingly, but that of the sixteenth and seventeenth centuries still all too well: in all these ages we see even minds of the first rank as if lamed by these false premises, and especially is all insight into the true character and activity of nature shut off to them. Throughout the entire Christian era theism has lain like an incubus on all intellectual, especially philosophical endeavour and has prevented or stunted all progress; and when anyone has possessed the rare elasticity of mind which alone can slip free of these fetters, his writings have been burned and sometimes their author with them, as happened to Bruno and Vanini. – But how completely paralysed *ordinary* minds are by this early metaphysical conditioning can be seen in its most lurid and ludicrous aspect when such a mind ventures to criticize a doctrine different from the one he himself holds. All you find him concerned to do as a rule is to demonstrate that its dogmas differ from those of his own: with that he believes in all simplicity he has proved the falsity of the other doctrine. It really never enters his head to pose the question which of the two might be true: his own articles of faith are to him certain *a priori*.

Demopheles So that is your higher viewpoint. I assure you there is a yet higher one. The saying *Primum vivere, deinde philosophari* [5] has a more comprehensive meaning than may at first sight appear. – What matters before all else is to restrain the rude and evil dispositions of the mass of the people and so prevent them from perpetrating acts of violence, cruelty and infamy and the more extreme forms of injustice: and if you delayed doing that until they had come to recognize and understand truth, you would infallibly have to wait for ever. For even supposing truth had already been discovered, they would be incapable of grasping it: they would still need to have it clothed in allegory, parable, myth. As Kant has said, there must always be a public standard of right and virtue, and this standard must indeed always be seen fluttering high in the breeze. In the last resort it is a matter of indifference which heraldic figure stands upon it, provided only it correctly indicates what is meant. Such an allegorical representation of truth is for mankind as a whole everywhere and always an answerable substitute for the truth itself, which is for ever inaccessible to it, and for philosophy in general, which it will never comprehend – quite apart from the fact that this changes every day and has never yet assumed a form which has won universal recognition. So you see, my dear Philalethes, practical aims take precedence over theoretical ones in every respect.

Philalethes This whole point of view is as misguided as it is nowadays universally praised and popular: which is why I now hasten to enter a protest against it. It is *untrue* that state, law and justice can be maintained only with the assistance of religion and its articles, and that the judiciary and the police

5. First live, then philosophize.

require it as their necessary complement for preserving public order. It is *untrue*, though it were reiterated a hundred times. For the ancients, and especially the Greeks, provide us with a factual and striking *instantia in contrarium*: they possessed nothing whatever of what we understand by *religion*. They had no sacred scriptures, and they had no dogmas which were taught, adherence to which was demanded of everybody, and which were imprinted on the minds of children. Nor did the administrators of their religion preach morals or worry about what people were doing or not doing. Absolutely not! The duties of the priests extended no further than temple ceremonial, prayers, hymns, sacrifices, processions, lustrations, and so forth, all of which has nothing to do with the moral improvement of the individual. The whole of so-called religion consisted rather in seeing that this or that god was provided with a temple in which his cult was carried on under the offices of the state, which cult was therefore at bottom a police matter. No man, apart from the functionaries involved, was in any way obliged to attend these ceremonies, or even to believe in the cult. No trace of a duty to believe in any dogma whatever is to be discovered in the whole of antiquity. Only if a man publicly denied the existence of the gods, or otherwise disparaged them, did he render himself liable to punishment: for then he affronted the state, which served them: but apart from this everyone was free to decide for himself how much he believed. Of the immortality of the soul and a life after death the ancients, far from having a dogmatically fixed conception, had no firm or clear conception at all; their ideas on these subjects were altogether loose, vacillating, indefinite and problematic, and each had his own; and their ideas about their gods were equally various, individual and vague. Thus the ancients really had no *religion* in our sense of the word. But did anarchy and lawlessness reign among them because they had no religion? did they not rather produce law and civic order to such purpose that it still remains as the basis of our own? was property not completely secure, even though it consisted in a large degree of slaves? And did this state of things not endure for well over a thousand years? – So I cannot acknowledge that religion has a practical objective, nor that it is indispensably necessary as the basis of all civil order. For if such were the case, then the sacred endeavour to attain to light and truth would appear at the least quixotic, and if it should venture to denounce the official faith as a usurper who had taken over the throne of truth and maintained its seat by perpetual deception, it would appear criminal.

Demophiles But religion is not antithetical to truth; for it itself teaches truth; only, because its field of action is not a narrow lecture-room but the whole world and all mankind, it has to adapt itself to the needs and abilities of a large and assorted public, and cannot present the truth naked. Religion is truth expressed in allegory and myth and thus made accessible and digestible to mankind at large: for mankind at large could never endure it pure and unalloyed, just as we cannot live on pure oxygen. The profound meaning and lofty goal of life can be revealed to the people and kept before their eyes only in *symbolical* form, because the people are not capable of grasping it literally. Philosophy, on the other hand, should, like the Eleusinian Mysteries, be reserved for the few and select.

Philalethes I understand: what it comes down to is that truth is to be clothed in lies. But that is an alliance which will ruin it: for what a dangerous weapon you place in a man's hands when you grant him the right to employ untruth as a vehicle for truth! If that is allowed, then I fear untruth will do more harm than the truth it carries will ever do good. If allegory would confess itself to be such then indeed I might not object: only, if it did that, it would forfeit all respect and consequently all effectiveness. It therefore has to put itself forward as true *sensu proprio*, whereas it is at the most true *sensu allegorico*. Here lies the incurable harm, the enduring evil which has always brought religion into conflict with the noble, unprejudiced endeavour to attain to pure truth, and which will always do so.

Demophiles Not at all: that too has been guarded against. For though religion may not openly confess its allegorical nature, it nonetheless gives sufficient indication of it.

Philalethes How does it do that?

Demopheles Through its mysteries. 'Mystery' is even at bottom the theological *terminus technicus* for religious allegory. All religions, moreover, have their mysteries. Properly speaking, a mystery is an obviously absurd dogma which nonetheless conceals a lofty truth in itself completely incomprehensible to the common understanding of the uncultivated mass of the people, who then absorb this truth thus disguised and take it on trust without being misled by the absurdity which is obvious to them too: thus they participate in the kernel of the matter in so far as it is possible for them to do so. You will understand better what I mean when I say that mystery is employed in philosophy too, as when, for example, Pascal,[6] who was pietist, mathematician and philosopher in one, says in this threefold capacity: God is everywhere centre and nowhere periphery. Malebranche[7] too has rightly said: *La liberté est un mystère.* – One could go further and assert that everything in religions is really mystery: for to impart truth *sensu proprio* to the people in its uncultivated state is absolutely impossible: all it is capable of is enlightenment through an allegorical reflexion of it. Naked truth does not belong before the eyes of the profane vulgar: it must appear before them heavily veiled. Hence it is quite unreasonable to require of a religion that it shall be true *sensu proprio.* Myth and allegory are its proper element: but under this unavoidable condition, imposed by the mental limitations of the great multitude, it offers sufficient satisfaction to the ineradicable metaphysical need of man, and takes the place of pure philosophical truth, which is infinitely difficult to attain and perhaps never will be attained.

Philalethes Oh yes, more or less as a wooden leg takes the place of a natural one: it substitutes for it, does duty for it as best it can, claims to be regarded as a natural leg, is artificially put together well or less well, and so on. The only difference is that, while a natural leg as a rule preceded the wooden one, religion has everywhere got the start on philosophy.

6. Blaise Pascal (1623–62).
7. Nicolas Malebranche (1638–1715), philosopher.

Demopheles That may be: but if you haven't got a natural leg a wooden one is very useful. You must bear in mind that the metaphysical need of man absolutely demands satisfaction, because the horizon of his thoughts must be closed and not remain unbounded. But man has as a rule no capacity for weighing reasons and then deciding between true and false; moreover, the labour which nature and its needs impose upon him leaves him no time for such inquiries, nor for the education they presuppose. In his case, therefore, there can be no question of conviction by reasons: he must be referred to belief and authority. Even if a really true philosophy had taken the place of religion, nine-tenths of mankind at the very least would receive it on authority, so that it too would be a matter of belief. Authority, however, can be established only by time and circumstance: it cannot be bestowed upon that which has only reasons in its favour. It must be allowed to that which has acquired it during the course of history, even if it is only an allegorical representation of truth. This representation, supported by authority, appeals first of all to the actual metaphysical predisposition of man, to the theoretical need which arises from the importunate enigma of our existence and from the consciousness that behind the world's physical plane there must be concealed a metaphysical, something unchanging which serves as a basis for the world's continual change; then, however, it appeals to the will, to the fears and hopes of mortals living in constant distress, for whom it accordingly creates gods and demons on whom they can call, whom they can appease, whom they can win over; finally, it appeals to the moral consciousness undeniably present in man, to which it lends external stay and confirmation, a support without which it would not easily be able to maintain itself in the struggle with so many temptations. It is precisely from this side that religion affords an inexhaustible source of consolation and comfort in the countless and great sufferings of life which does not desert men even in the hour of death but rather only then reveals its full efficacy. Religion may thus be compared to one who takes a blind man by the hand and leads him, since he cannot see for himself and the sole point is that he should arrive at his destination, not that he should see all there is to see.

Philalethes This last aspect is certainly the strong point of religion. If it is a *fraus*, it is a *pia fraus*[8]: that is undeniable. But this makes a priest into a curious cross between a deceiver and a moralist. For they durst not teach the real truth, as you have quite rightly explained, even if they knew it, which they do not. So that a true philosophy is possible, but not a true religion: I mean true in the proper meaning of the word, and not merely metaphorically or allegorically true in the way you have described; in that sense all religions would be true, only in differing degrees. In any event, it is quite in keeping with the inextricable tangle of weal and woe, honesty and deceit, goodness and badness, nobility and baseness which the world as a rule presents us with that the weightiest, loftiest and most sacred truth can make its appearance only when adulterated with a lie, has indeed to borrow strength from a lie as from something which makes a stronger impression on mankind, and must be ushered in by a lie in the form of revelation. One could even regard this fact as the distinguishing mark of the moral world. However, let us not abandon the hope that mankind will one day reach the point of maturity and education at which it is capable of on the one hand producing and on the other receiving true philosophy. *Simplex sigillum veri*[9]: naked truth must be so simple and intelligible that it can be imparted to everyone in its true shape without adulterating it with myths and fables (a mass of lies) – that is, without disguising it as *religion*.

Demopheles You have an inadequate idea of how limited the capacity of most people is.

Philalethes It was merely a hope I was expressing: but it is a hope which I cannot give up. If it were fulfilled it would of course drive religion from the place which it has so long occupied in its stead but by that very means kept open for it. Religion would have fulfilled its task and run its course: it could then release the race it has conducted to its majority and itself pass peacefully away. This would be the euthanasia of

8. Pious fraud.   9. Simplicity is the seal of truth.

religion. But as long as it lives it has two faces: one the face of truth, the other the face of deception. You will love it or detest it according to whether you keep one or the other face in view. You have to regard it as a necessary evil, its necessity deriving from the wretched imbecility of the majority of mankind, which is incapable of understanding truth and therefore, in this pressing case, requires a substitute for it.

Demopheles Hold to that conclusion, then, and bear always in mind that religion has two sides. If it cannot be justified from the theoretical, that is to say intellectual side, from the moral side it proves to be the sole means of guiding, controlling and appeasing this race of animals endowed with reason whose kinship with the ape does not exclude kinship with the tiger. If you consider religion in this light and remember that its aims are above all practical and only secondarily theoretical, it will appear to you as worthy of the highest respect.

Philalethes Which respect would rest ultimately on the principle that the end sanctifies the means. I have no inclination for a compromise founded on that basis. Religion may be an excellent means of taming and training the perverse, obtuse and wicked biped race: but in the eyes of the friend of truth every fraud, however pious, is still a fraud. A pack of lies would be a strange means of inducing virtue. The flag to which I have sworn allegiance is truth: I shall stay faithful to it everywhere and, regardless of the outcome, fight for light and truth. If I see the religions in the ranks of the enemy ...

Demopheles But you won't find them there! Religion is no deception: it is true and is the most important of all truths. But because, as I have already said, its doctrines are of so lofty a kind that the multitude could not grasp them directly; because, I say, its light would blind the common eye; it appears veiled in allegory and teaches that which, while not strictly true in itself, is true in respect of the lofty meaning contained within it: and thus understood, religion is truth.

Philalethes That would be fair enough – if it could only venture to present itself as true in a merely allegorical sense. But it comes forward claiming to be true in the strict and proper sense of the word: therein lies the deception, and here is the point at which the friend of truth must oppose it.

Demopheles But that is *conditio sine qua non*.[10] If religion were to admit that it was only the allegorical meaning of its doctrine which was true this would rob it of all efficacy; through such rigorousness its incalculably beneficial influence on the heart and morality of men would be lost. You ought to guard against letting your theoretical cavilling discredit in the eyes of the people and finally wrest from them something which is an inexhaustible source of consolation and comfort, and which they need so much, indeed with their hard lot need more than we do: for this reason alone it ought to be inviolable.

Philalethes With *that* argument you could have driven Luther from the field when he attacked the sale of indulgences. – Truth, my friend, truth alone holds firm, endures and stays steadfast: truth's consolation is the only solid consolation: it is the indestructible diamond.

Demopheles Yes, if you had truth in your pocket, and could favour us with it on demand. But all you have is metaphysical systems about which nothing is certain but the head-cudgelling they cost. Before you deprive someone of something you must have something better to put in its place.

Philalethes Oh, to have to go on hearing that said! To free a man from an error is not to deprive him of anything but to give him something: for the knowledge that a thing is false is a piece of truth. No error is harmless: sooner or later it will bring misfortune to him who harbours it. Therefore deceive no one, but rather confess ignorance of what you do not know, and leave each man to devise his own articles of faith for himself.

Demopheles A particularism of that sort is totally opposed to human nature and would consequently be the end of all social order. Man is an *animal metaphysicum*, that is, his metaphysical need is more urgent than any other; he thus conceives life above all according to its metaphysical meaning and wants to see everything in the light of that. Consequently, and however

10. Indispensable condition.

strange it may sound in view of the uncertainty of all dogma, agreement on fundamental metaphysical views is the chief thing for man, because genuine and lasting social union is possible only among those who do agree on these. The social structure, the state, will stand quite firm only when it is founded on a universally recognized metaphysical system. Such a system can naturally be only one of folk-metaphysics, that is, religion; which is then fused with the state constitution and with every social manifestation of the people's life, as it also is with every solemn act of private life. The social structure could hardly exist at all if religion did not lend weight to the government's authority and the ruler's dignity.

Philalethes Oh yes, princes use the Lord God as a bogy to get their grown-up children to bed when nothing else will any longer serve; which is why they value him so highly. Very well; but I would advise every ruler to sit down every half-year on a certain fixed date and carefully read the fifteenth chapter of the First Book of Samuel, so as always to have in mind what it means to use the altar to support the throne. Moreover, since that *ultima ratio theologorum* [11], the stake, has gone out of use the effectiveness of this means of government has much diminished. For, as you know, religions are like glow-worms: they need darkness in order to shine. A certain degree of general ignorance is the condition for the existence of any religion, the element in which alone it is able to live. Perhaps the day so often prophesied will soon come when religions will depart from European man like a nurse whose care the child has outgrown and which henceforth comes under the instruction of a tutor. For articles of faith based on nothing but authority, miracles and revelation are beyond doubt short-term aids appropriate only to the childhood of mankind: and it must be admitted that a race which, according to all the indications provided by physical and historical data, is at present no older than one hundred times the life of a man of sixty, is still in its first childhood.

Demopheles Oh if, instead of prophesying with unconcealed

11. Final argument of theology.

delight the end of Christianity, you would only consider how infinitely great a debt European man owes to it! He received from Christianity an outlook previously unfamiliar to him, an outlook deriving from knowledge of the fundamental truth that life cannot be an end in itself, but that the true end of our existence lies beyond life. For the Greeks and Romans had placed it entirely *within* life, in which respect at any rate they can be called blind heathen. All their virtues consequently can be traced back to qualities serviceable to the community, to useful qualities, and Aristotle says naïvely: 'Those virtues must necessarily be the greatest which are the most useful to others.' Christianity liberated European man from this exclusive involvement in an ephemeral and uncertain existence. The Greeks and Romans had forgotten the serious, true and profound significance of life: they lived heedlessly, like grownup children, until Christianity came and called them back to life's earnestness.

Philalethes And to judge how it succeeded we have only to compare antiquity with the Middle Ages which followed it, the age of Pericles, say, with the fourteenth century. You would hardly think you were dealing with the same species. In the former the fairest unfolding of humanity, a splendid state structure, wise laws, a carefully balanced legal administration, rationally regulated freedom, all the arts, together with poetry and philosophy, at their peak, creating works which after thousands of years still stand as unequalled models of their kind, almost as the productions of higher beings whom we can never hope to emulate, and at the same time life beautified by the noblest social fellowship such as we see reflected in *The Symposium* of Xenophon.[12] And now look at the latter age, if you are able to. Look at the age when the Church had fettered the minds and forced the bodies of mankind, so that knights and priests might lay all the drudgery of life on their common beasts of burden, the third estate. Here you find *force majeure*, feudalism and fanaticism in intimate alliance, and in their train

12. Xenophon (born *c.* 430 B.C.), soldier and writer. *The Symposium* is a dialogue in which Socrates figures.

hideous ignorance and darkness of mind, and in consequence intolerance, quarrelling over beliefs, religious wars, crusades, persecution of heretics and inquisitions; while social fellowship took the form of a knightly chivalry compounded of brutality and foppishness, with grotesqueries and humbug pedantically reduced to a system, with degrading superstition and apish veneration of women. The ancients were unquestionably less cruel than the Middle Ages; and they were, moreover, very tolerant, laid great stress on justice, frequently sacrificed themselves for their country, and displayed such nobility of every kind and so genuine a humanity that to this very day an acquaintanceship with their thoughts and actions is called a study of the humanities. Their tolerance of pederasty, which is certainly reprehensible and the principal reproach now made against the morality of the ancients, is a trifling thing compared with the Christian abominations I have mentioned, and that this practice is less evident now by no means implies that it is that much less prevalent. All things considered, can you maintain that mankind has really been made morally better by Christianity?

Demopheles If the results have not everywhere corresponded to the purity and truth of the doctrine it may be because this doctrine has been too noble, too exalted for mankind, and its goal has therefore been placed too high: it was certainly easier to comply with heathen morality, as it is with Mohammedan. What is most exalted is always most open to abuse and imposture; so that these lofty doctrines too have sometimes served as a pretext for the most atrocious proceedings and acts of wickedness.

Philalethes It would really be an extremely useful inquiry to try to make a completely impartial and accurate assessment of the advantages derived from religion compared with the disadvantages which have attended it. But that would require a much greater quantity of historical and psychological data than we two have at our command. Academies could make it the subject of a prize essay.

Demopheles They will take care not to do so.

Philalethes I am surprised you should say that: for it is a bad sign for religion. – If only a statistician could tell us first of all how many crimes are refrained from each year from religious motives and how many from other motives. There would be very few of the former. For when a man feels tempted to commit a crime, then you can depend on it that the first thing he thinks of in opposition to the idea is the punishment appointed for it and the probability of its falling upon him; the second consideration is the risk to his honour. On these two objections he will, if I am not mistaken, ponder for hours before religious considerations so much as occur to him. If, however, he gets over these two first bulwarks against crime, I believe that religion *alone* will very rarely hold him back.

Demopheles But I believe it will do so very often, especially when its influence is already operative through the medium of custom, so that a man immediately shrinks from committing any great act of wickedness. Early impressions are enduring.

Philalethes Suppose a public proclamation were suddenly made at this moment repealing all laws relating to crime: I fancy neither you nor I would have the courage even to go home alone under the protection of religious motives. If, on the other hand, all religions were in the same way declared untrue, we should go on living as before under the protection of the law alone without any special precautions. – But I will go further, and say that religions have very frequently had a decidedly harmful influence on morality. It may be asserted as a generalization that what is given to God is taken from men, inasmuch as it is very easy to substitute adulation of the former for decent behaviour towards the latter. In every religion, faith, temple ceremonies and rites of all kinds soon come to be pronounced of more immediate interest to the divine will than moral actions; indeed, the former, especially when they are bound up with the emoluments of the priests, gradually come to be regarded as a substitute for the latter: animal sacrifices, or the saying of masses, or the founding of chapels, or the erection of wayside crosses, soon come to be the most meritorious works, so that they atone for even the gravest crimes, as do penances, subjection to priestly authority, confessions, pilgrimages, donations to the temples and their priests, the building of monasteries, and the like, whereby the priests finally appear as virtually no more than go-betweens in a trade with bribable gods. And even if it doesn't go as far as that, where is the religion whose adherents do not consider at any rate prayers, hymns and various acts of devotion as at least a partial substitute for moral conduct? – But to return to the main point: you are certainly right to urge the strong metaphysical need of mankind, but religion appears to me not so much the satisfaction as the abuse of this need. We have seen that at any rate as regards the advancement of morality its utility is in great part problematic, while its disadvantages and especially the atrocities which have followed in its train are patently obvious. The matter bears another complexion, to be sure, if we consider the utility of religion as a prop for thrones, for where these are held by the grace of God altar and throne stand in the closest association: every wise prince who loves his throne and his family will consequently always set himself up before his people as a model of true religiousness.

Demopheles Well, after all the trouble I have taken I am sorry not to have altered your attitude towards religion: on the other hand, I can assure you that nothing *you* have adduced has succeeded in shaking my conviction of its high value and necessity.

Philalethes I believe you: for, as it says in *Hudibras*:

> A man convinced against his will
> Is of the same opinion still.

But I console myself with the thought that, with controversies and mineral baths alike, the only real effect is the after-effect.

Demopheles Then let me wish you a pleasant after-effect.

Philalethes You might have your wish if only my stomach could digest a certain Spanish proverb.

Demopheles Which is?

Philalethes Detras de la cruz está el Diablo.

Demopheles Which is in English?

Philalethes Behind the Cross stands the Devil.

Demopheles Come, don't let us part with sarcasms. Let us see rather that, like Janus – or better, like Yama, the Brahmin god of death – religion has two faces, one very friendly, one very gloomy: you have had your eyes fixed on one face, I have had mine fixed on the other.

Philalethes You are right, old man!

APHORISMS

ON PHILOSOPHY AND THE INTELLECT

1

THE fundament upon which all our knowledge and learning rests is the inexplicable. It is to this that every explanation, through few or many intermediate stages, leads; as the plummet touches the bottom of the sea now at a greater depth, now at a less, but is bound to reach it somewhere sooner or later. The study of this inexplicable devolves upon metaphysics.

2

For *intellect in the service of will*, that is to say in practical use, there exist only *individual things*; for intellect engaged in art and science, that is to say active for its own sake, there exist only *universals*, entire kinds, species, classes, *ideas* of things. Even the sculptor, in depicting the individual, seeks to depict the idea, the species. The reason for this is that *will* aims directly only at individual things, which are its true objective, for only they possess empirical reality. Concepts, classes, kinds, on the other hand, can become its objective only very indirectly. That is why the ordinary man has no sense for general truths, and why the genius, on the contrary, overlooks and neglects what is individual : to the genius the enforced occupation with the individual as such which constitutes the stuff of practical life is a burdensome drudgery.

3

The two main requirements for philosophizing are : firstly, to have the courage not to keep any question back; and secondly, to attain a clear consciousness of anything that *goes without saying* so as to comprehend it as a problem. Finally, the mind must, if it is really to philosophize, also be truly disengaged : it must prosecute no particular goal or aim, and thus be free from the enticement of will, but devote itself undividedly to the instruction which the perceptible world and its own consciousness imparts to it.

4

The *poet* presents the imagination with images from life and human characters and situations, sets them all in motion and leaves it to the beholder to let these images take his thoughts as far as his mental powers will permit. That is why he is able to engage men of the most differing capabilities, indeed fools and sages together. The *philosopher*, on the other hand, presents not life itself but the finished thoughts which he has abstracted from it and then demands that the reader should think precisely as, and precisely as far as, he himself thinks. That is why his public is so small. The poet can thus be compared with one who presents flowers, the philosopher with one who presents their essence.

5

An odd and unworthy definition of philosophy, which however even Kant gives, is that it is a science *composed only of concepts*. For the entire property of a concept consists of nothing more than what has been begged and borrowed from perceptual knowledge, which is the true and inexhaustible source of all insight. So that a true philosophy cannot be spun out of mere abstract concepts, but has to be founded on observation and experience, inner and outer. Nor will anything worthwhile be achieved in philosophy by synthesizing experiments with concepts such as have been performed so often in the past but especially by the sophists of our own day – I mean by Fichte and Schelling and even more offensively by Hegel, and in the field of ethics by Schleiermacher.[1] Philosophy, just as much as art and poetry, must have its source in perceptual comprehension of the

1. Johann Gottlieb Fichte (1762–1814), Friedrich Wilhelm Joseph von Schelling (1775–1854), Georg Wilhelm Friedrich Hegel (1770–1831): German philosophers, the most influential of their age and the subject of constant

world: nor, however much the head needs to remain on top, ought it to be so cold-blooded a business that the whole man, heart and head, is not finally involved and affected through and through. Philosophy is not algebra: on the contrary, Vauvenargues[2] was right when he said: *Les grandes pensées viennent du cœur.*

6

Mere subtlety may qualify you as a sceptic but not as a philosopher. On the other hand, scepticism is in philosophy what the Opposition is in Parliament; it is just as beneficial, and indeed necessary. It rests everywhere on the fact that philosophy is not capable of producing the kind of evidence mathematics produces.

7

A *dictate of reason* is the name we give to certain propositions which we hold true without investigation and of which we think ourselves so firmly convinced we should be incapable of seriously testing them even if we wanted to, since we should then have to call them provisionally in doubt. We credit these propositions so completely because when we first began to speak and think we continually had them recited to us and they were thus implanted in us; so that the habit of thinking them is as old as the habit of thinking as such and we can no longer separate the two.

8

People never weary of reproaching metaphysics with the very small progress it has made compared with the very great progress of the physical sciences. But what other science has been hampered at all times by having an antagonist *ex officio*, a public prosecutor, a king's champion in full armour against it?

---

attack by Schopenhauer. Friedrich Ernst Daniel Schleiermacher (1768–1834), theologian: when Schopenhauer attacks 'Rationalism' in religion it is Schleiermacher he has in mind.

2. Luc de Clapiers, Marquis de Vauvenargues (1715–47), 'moralist' in the French sense.

Metaphysics will never put forth its full powers so long as it is expected to accommodate itself to dogma. The various religions have taken possession of the metaphysical tendency of mankind, partly by paralysing it through imprinting their dogmas upon it in the earliest years, partly by forbidding and proscribing all free and uninhibited expression of it; so that free investigation of man's most important and interesting concern, of his existence itself, has been in part indirectly hampered, in part made subjectively impossible by the paralysis referred to; and in this way his most sublime tendency has been put in chains.

9

The discovery of truth is prevented most effectively, not by the false appearance things present and which mislead into error, nor directly by weakness of the reasoning powers, but by preconceived opinion, by prejudice, which as a pseudo *a priori* stands in the path of truth and is then like a contrary wind driving a ship away from land, so that sail and rudder labour in vain.

10

Every *general* truth is related to specific truths as gold is to silver, inasmuch as it can be converted into a considerable number of specific truths which follow from it in the same way as a gold coin can be converted into small change.

11

From *one* proposition nothing more can follow than what is already contained in it, i.e. than what it itself implies when its meaning is exhausted; but from *two* propositions, if they are joined together as premises of a syllogism, more can follow than is contained in either of them taken individually – just as a body formed by chemical combination exhibits qualities possessed by none of its constituents. That logical conclusions possess value derives from this fact.

12

What light is to the outer physical world intellect is to the inner world of consciousness. For intellect is related to will, and thus also to the organism, which is nothing other than will regarded objectively, in approximately the same way as light is to a combustible body and the oxygen in combination with which it ignites. And as light is the purer the less it is involved with the smoke of the burning body, so also is intellect the purer the more completely it is separated from the will which engendered it. In a bolder metaphor one could even say: Life is known to be a process of combustion; intellect is the light produced by this process.

13

The simplest unprejudiced self-observation, combined with the facts of anatomy, leads to the conclusion that intellect, like its objectivization the brain, is, together with its dependent sense-apparatus, nothing other than a very intense receptivity to influences from without and does not constitute our original and intrinsic being; thus that intellect is not that in us which in a plant is motive power or in a stone weight and chemical forces: it is *will* alone which appears in these forms. Intellect is that in us which in a plant is merely receptivity to external influences, to physical and chemical action and whatever else may help or hinder it to grow and thrive; but in us this receptivity has risen to such a pitch of intensity that by virtue of it the entire objective world, the world as idea, appears; and this, consequently, is how its objectivization originates. It will help to make all this more vivid if you imagine the world without any animal life on it. There will then be nothing on it capable of perceiving it, and therefore it will actually have no objective existence at all. Now imagine a number of plants shooting up out of the ground close beside one another. All kinds of things will begin to operate on them, such as air, wind, the pressure of one plant against another, moisture, cold, light, warmth, electricity, etc. Now imagine the receptivity of these plants to influences of this kind intensified more and more: it will finally become sensation, accompanied by the capacity to refer sensation to its cause, and at last perception: whereupon the world will be there, appearing in space, time and causal connexion – yet it will still be merely the result of external influences on the receptivity of the plants. This pictorial representation brings home very well the merely phenomenal existence of the external world and makes it comprehensible: for no one, surely, would care to assert that a state of affairs which consists of perceptions originating in nothing but relations between external influences and active receptivity represents the truly objective, inner and original constitution of all those natural forces assumed to be acting on the plants; that it represents, that is to say, the world of things in themselves. This picture can thus make it comprehensible to us why the realm of the human intellect should have such narrow boundaries, as Kant demonstrates it has in the *Critique of Pure Reason*.

14

That you should write down valuable ideas that occur to you as soon as possible goes without saying: we sometimes forget even what we have done, so how much more what we have thought. Thoughts, however, come not when *we* but when *they* want. On the other hand, it is better not to copy down what we have received finished and complete from without, what we have merely learned and what can in any case be discovered again in books: for to copy something down is to consign it to forgetfulness. You should deal sternly and despotically with your memory, so that it does not unlearn obedience; if, for example, you cannot call something to mind, a line of poetry or a word perhaps, you should not go and look it up in a book, but periodically plague your memory with it for weeks on end until your memory has done its duty. For the longer you have had to rack your brains for something the more firmly will it stay once you have got it.

15

The *quality* of our thoughts (their formal value) comes from within, their *direction*, and thus their matter, from without; so that what we are thinking at any given moment is the product of two fundamentally different factors. Consequently, the object of thought is to the mind only what the plectrum is to the lyre: which is why the same sight inspires such very different thoughts in differing heads.

16

How very paltry and limited the normal human intellect is, and how little lucidity there is in the human consciousness, may be judged from the fact that, despite the ephemeral brevity of human life, the uncertainty of our existence and the countless enigmas which press upon us from all sides, everyone does not continually and ceaselessly philosophize, but that only the rarest of exceptions do so. The rest live their lives away in this dream not very differently from the animals, from which they are in the end distinguished only by their ability to provide for a few years ahead. If they should ever feel any metaphysical need, it is taken care of from above and in advance by the various religions; and these, whatever they may be like, suffice.

17

One might almost believe that half our thinking takes place unconsciously. Usually we arrive at a conclusion without having clearly thought about the premises which lead to it. This is already evident from the fact that sometimes an occurrence whose consequences we can in no way foresee, still less clearly estimate its possible influence on our own affairs, will nonetheless exercise an unmistakable influence on our whole mood and will change it from cheerful to sad or from sad to cheerful: this can only be the result of unconscious rumination. It is even more obvious in the following: I have familiarized myself with the factual data of a theoretical or practical problem; I do not think about it again, yet often a few days later the answer to the problem will come into my mind entirely of its own accord; the operation which has produced it, however, remains as much a mystery to me as that of an adding-machine: what has occurred is, again, unconscious rumination. – One might almost venture the physiological hypothesis that conscious thinking takes place on the surface of the brain, unconscious thinking inside it.

18

Considering the monotony and consequent insipidity of life one would find it unendurably tedious after any considerable length of time, were it not for the continual advance of knowledge and insight and the acquisition of even better and clearer understanding of all things, which is partly the fruit of experience, partly the result of the changes we ourselves undergo through the different stages of life by which our point of view is to a certain extent being continually altered, whereby things reveal to us sides we did not yet know. In this way, despite the decline in our mental powers, *dies diem docet*[3] still holds indefatigably true and gives life an ever-renewed fascination, in that what is identical continually appears as something new and different.

19

It is quite natural that we should adopt a defensive and negative attitude towards every new opinion concerning something on which we have already an opinion of our own. For it forces its way as an enemy into the previously closed system of our own convictions, shatters the calm of mind we have attained through this system, demands renewed efforts of us and declares our former efforts to have been in vain. A truth which retrieves us from error is consequently to be compared with a physic, as much for its bitter and repellent taste as for the fact that it takes effect not at the moment it is imbibed but only some time afterwards.

Thus, if we see the individual obstinately clinging to his

3. 'The day teaches the day' – there is something new every day.

errors, with the mass of men it is even worse: once they have acquired an opinion, experience and instruction can labour for centuries against it and labour in vain. So that there exist certain universally popular and firmly accredited errors which countless numbers contentedly repeat every day: I have started a list of them which others might like to continue.

1. Suicide is a cowardly act.

2. He who mistrusts others is himself dishonest.

3. Worth and genius are unfeignedly modest.

4. The insane are exceedingly unhappy.

5. Philosophizing can be learned, but not philosophy. (The opposite is true.)

6. It is easier to write a good tragedy than a good comedy.

7. A little philosophy leads away from God, a lot of it leads back to him – repeated after Francis Bacon.

8. Knowledge is power. The devil it is! One man can have a great deal of knowledge without its giving him the least power, while another possesses supreme authority but next to no knowledge.

Most of these are repeated parrot fashion without much thought being given to them and merely because when people first heard them said they found them very wise-sounding.

20

Intellect is a magnitude of intensity, not a magnitude of extension: which is why in this respect one man can confidently take on ten thousand and a thousand fools do not make one wise man.

21

What the pathetic commonplace heads with which the world is crammed really lack are two closely related faculties: that of forming judgements and that of producing ideas of their own. But these are lacking to a degree which he who is not one of them cannot easily conceive, so that he cannot easily conceive the dolefulness of their existence. It is this deficiency, however, which explains on one hand the poverty of the scribbling which in all nations passes itself off to its contemporaries as their literature, and on the other the fate that overtakes true and genuine men who appear among such people. All genuine thought and art is to a certain extent an attempt to put big heads on small people: so it is no wonder the attempt does not always come off. For a writer to afford enjoyment always demands a certain *harmony* between his way of thinking and that of the reader; and the enjoyment will be the greater the more perfect this harmony is: so that a great mind will fully and completely enjoy only another great mind. It is for this same reason that bad or mediocre writers excite disgust and revulsion in thinking heads: and even conversation with most people has the same effect – one is conscious of the inadequacy and *disharmony* every step of the way.

22

The life of the *plants* consists in simple *existence*: so that their enjoyment of life is a purely and absolutely subjective, torpid contentment. With the *animals* there enters *knowledge*: but it is still entirely restricted to what serves their own motivation, and indeed their most immediate motivation. That is why they too find complete contentment in simple existence and why it suffices to fill their entire lives; so that they can pass many hours completely inactive without feeling discontented or impatient, although they are not thinking but merely looking. Only in the very cleverest animals such as dogs and apes does the need for activity, and with that boredom, make itself felt; which is why they enjoy playing, and why they amuse themselves by gazing at passers-by; in which respect they are in a class with those human window-gazers who stare at us everywhere but only when one notices they are students really arouse our indignation.

Only in man has *knowledge* – i.e. the consciousness of other things, in antithesis to mere self-consciousness – reached a high degree and, with the appearance of the reasoning faculty, risen to thought. As a consequence of this his life can, besides simple existence, be filled by *knowledge* as such, which is to a certain extent a second existence outside oneself in other beings and things. With man too, however, knowledge is mostly restricted to what serves his own motivation, although this now includes motivations less immediate which, when taken together, are called 'practical knowledge'. On the other hand, he usually has no more *free*, i.e. purposeless, knowledge than is engendered by curiosity and the need for diversion; yet this kind of knowledge does exist in every man, even if only to this extent. In the meantime, when motivation is quiescent, the life of man is to a large extent filled by simple *existence*, to which fact the tremendous amount of lounging about that goes on and the commonness of that kind of sociability which consists chiefly in mere togetherness, without any conversation, or at the most very scanty conversation, bear witness. Indeed, most people have – in their hearts even if not consciously – as the supreme guide and maxim of their conduct the resolve *to get by with the least possible expenditure of thought*, because to them thinking is hard and burdensome. Consequently, they think only as much as their trade or business makes absolutely necessary, and then again as much as is demanded by their various pastimes – which is what their conversation is just as much as their play; but both must be so ordered that they can be tackled with a *minimum* of thought.

Only where intellect exceeds the measure needed for living does knowledge become more or less an end in itself. It is consequently a quite abnormal event if in some man intellect deserts its natural vocation – that of serving the will by perceiving mere relations between things – in order to occupy itself purely objectively. But it is precisely this which is the origin of art, poetry and philosophy, which are therefore produced by an organ not originally intended for that purpose. For intellect is fundamentally a hard-working factory-hand whom his demanding master, the will, keeps busy from morn to night. But if this hard-driven serf should once happen to do some of his work voluntarily during his free time, on his own initiative and without any object but the work itself, simply for his own satisfaction and enjoyment – then this is a genuine work of art, indeed, if pushed to an extreme, a work of genius.

Such a purely objective employment of the intellect, as well as lying behind all artistic, poetical and philosophical achievement of the higher kind, also lies behind all purely scientific achievement in general, is already present in purely scientific study and learning, likewise in any free reflection (i.e. reflection not involved with personal interest) upon any subject whatever. It is the same thing, indeed, which inspires even mere conversation if its theme is a purely objective one, i.e. is not related in any way to the interest, and consequently the will of those taking part in it. Every such purely objective employment of the intellect compares with its subjective employment – i.e. employment in regard to personal interest, however indirectly – as dancing does with walking: for, like dancing, it is the purposeless expenditure of excess energy. On the other hand, the subjective employment of intellect is, of course, the natural one, since intellect arose merely in order to serve will. It is involved not merely in work and the personal drives, but also in all conversation concerning personal affairs and material matters in general; in eating, drinking and other pleasures; in everything pertaining to earning a livelihood; and in utilitarian concerns of every sort. Most men, to be sure, are incapable of any other employment of their intellect, because with them it is merely a tool in service of their will and is entirely consumed by this service, without any remainder. It is this that makes them so arid, so brutishly earnest and incapable of objective conversation; just as the shortness of the bonds joining intellect to will is visible in their face. The impression of narrow-mindedness which often emerges from it in such a depressing fashion is, in fact, only the outward sign of the narrow limitation of their total stock of knowledge to the affairs of their own will. One can see that here there is just as much intellect as a given will requires for its ends and no more: hence the vulgarity of their aspect; and hence also the fact that their intellect subsides into inactivity the moment their will ceases to drive it. They take an *objective* interest in nothing whatever. Their attention, not to speak of their mind, is engaged by nothing that does not bear some relation, or at least some possible relation, to their own person: otherwise their interest is not aroused. They are not noticeably stimulated even by wit or humour; they hate rather everything that demands the slightest thought. Coarse buffooneries at most excite them to laughter: apart from that they are earnest brutes – and all because they are capable of only *subjective* interest. It is precisely this which makes card-playing the most appropriate amusement for them – card-playing for money: because this does not remain in the sphere of mere knowledge, as stage plays, music, conversation, etc., do, but sets in motion the *will* itself, the primary element which exists everywhere. For the rest they are, from their first breath to their last, tradesmen, life's born drudges. All their pleasures are sensuous: they have no feeling for any other kind of pleasure. Talk to them about business, but not about anything else. To be sociable with them is to be degraded. On the other hand, conversation between two people who are capable of some sort of purely *objective* employment of their intellect is a free play of intellectual energy, though the matter be never so insubstantial and amount to no more than jesting. Such a conversation is in fact like two or more dancing together: while the other sort is like marching side-by-side or one behind the other merely in order to arrive somewhere.

Now this tendency towards a free and thus abnormal employment of the intellect, together with the capacity for it, attains in the *genius* the point at which knowledge becomes the main thing, the *aim* of the whole of life; his own existence, on the other hand, declines to a subsidiary thing, a mere *means*; so that the normal relationship is completely reversed. Consequently, the genius lives on the whole more in the rest of the world, by virtue of his knowledge and comprehension of it, than in his own person. The entirely abnormal enhancement of his cognitive powers robs him of the possibility of filling up his time with mere *existence* and its aims: his mind needs to be constantly and vigorously occupied. He thus lacks that composure in traversing the broad scenes of everyday life and that easy absorption in them which is granted to ordinary men. So that genius is for the ordinary practical living appropriate to normal mental powers an ill endowment and, like every abnormality, an impediment: for with this intensifying of the intellectual powers, intuitive comprehension of the outside world achieves so great a degree of objective clarity and furnishes so much more than is requisite for serving the will that such an abundance becomes a downright hindrance to this service, inasmuch as to contemplate given phenomena in themselves and for their own sake constantly detracts from the contemplation of their connexions with the individual will and with one another and consequently disturbs and obstructs any clear comprehension of these connexions. For the service of the will an entirely superficial contemplation of things suffices, a contemplation which furnishes no more than their bearing on whatever aims we may have and whatever may be associated with these aims, and consequently consists of nothing but relationships, with the greatest possible degree of blindness towards everything else: an objective and complete comprehension of the nature of things enfeebles knowledge of this sort and throws it into disorder.

23

The difference between the genius and the normal intelligence is, to be sure, only a *quantitative* one, in so far as it is only a difference of degree: one is nonetheless tempted to regard it as a *qualitative* one when one considers how normal men, despite their individual diversity, all think along certain common lines, so that they are frequently in unanimous agreement over judgements which are, in fact, false. This goes so far that they have certain basic views which are held in all ages and continually reiterated, while the great minds of every age have, openly or secretly, opposed these views.

24

A genius is a man in whose head the *world as idea* has attained a greater degree of clarity and is present more distinctly; and since the weightiest and profoundest insight is furnished not by painstaking observation of what is separate and individual but by the intensity with which the whole is comprehended, mankind can expect from him the profoundest sort of instruction. Genius can thus also be defined as an exceptionally clear consciousness of things and therefore also of their antithesis, one's own self. Mankind looks up to one who is thus gifted for disclosures about things and about its own nature.

25

If you want to earn the gratitude of your own age you must keep in step with it. But if you do that you will produce nothing great. If you have something great in view you must address yourself to posterity: only then, to be sure, you will probably remain unknown to your contemporaries; you will be like a man compelled to spend his life on a desert island and there toiling to erect a memorial so that future seafarers shall know he once existed.

26

Talent works for money and fame: the motive which moves *genius* to productivity is, on the other hand, less easy to determine. It isn't money, for genius seldom gets any. It isn't fame: fame is too uncertain and, more closely considered, of too little worth. Nor is it strictly for its own pleasure, for the great exertion involved almost outweighs the pleasure. It is rather an instinct of a unique sort by virtue of which the individual possessed of genius is impelled to express what he has seen and felt in enduring works without being conscious of any further motivation. It takes place, by and large, with the same sort of necessity as a tree brings forth fruit, and demands of the world no more than a soil on which the individual can flourish. More closely considered, it is as if in such an individual the will to live, as the spirit of the human species, had become conscious of having, by a rare accident, attained for a brief span of time to a greater clarity of intellect, and now endeavours to acquire at any rate the results, the products of this clear thought and vision for the whole species, which is indeed also the intrinsic being of this individual, so that their light may continue to illumine the darkness and stupor of the ordinary human consciousness. It is from this that there arises that instinct which impels genius to labour in solitude to complete its work without regard for reward, applause or sympathy, but neglectful rather even of its own well-being and thinking more of posterity than of the age it lives in, which could only lead it astray. To make its work, as a sacred trust and the true fruit of its existence, the property of mankind, laying it down for a posterity better able to appreciate it: this becomes for genius a goal more important than any other, a goal for which it wears the crown of thorns that shall one day blossom into a laurel-wreath. Its striving to complete and safeguard its work is just as resolute as that of the insect to safeguard its eggs and provide for the brood it will never live to see: it deposits its eggs where it knows they will one day find life and nourishment, and dies contented.

ON ETHICS

1

THAT the world has no ethical significance but only a physical one is the greatest and most pernicious of errors, the fundamental error, the intrinsically *perverse* view, and is probably at bottom also that which faith has personified as the Anti-Christ. Nevertheless, and despite all the religions, which all assert the opposite and seek to demonstrate it in mythical form, this fundamental error never quite dies out on earth but raises its head again and again until general indignation again and again compels it to hide it.

2

As a consequence of their profounder ethical and metaphysical insight, the *Buddhists* start not with cardinal virtues but with cardinal vices, as the antitheses or negations of which the cardinal virtues first appear. According to J. J. Schmidt's *Geschichte der Ostmongolen* the Buddhist cardinal vices are lust, sloth, wrath and avarice, although pride should probably stand in place of sloth, as it does in the *Lettres édifiantes et curieuses* (edition of 1819), where, however, envy or hatred is added as a fifth. The sufis[1] too lay down the same cardinal vices, arranged very strikingly in couples, so that lust is paired with avarice and wrath with pride. We find lust, wrath and avarice already laid down as cardinal vices in the *Bhagavad Gita*, which is evidence of the extreme antiquity of the doctrine. These three cardinal vices likewise appear in the *Prabodha-Chandrodaya,* an allegorical philosophical drama very important for the Vedanta, where they are the three commanders in the service of King Passion in his war against King Reason. It would follow that

1. Mystical sect within Mohammedism.

the cardinal virtues antithetical to these cardinal vices are chastity and generosity, together with gentleness and humility.

If you now compare with these profound basic concepts of oriental ethics the celebrated and thousand-times reiterated Platonic cardinal virtues, justice, bravery, moderation, and wisdom, you will find the latter do not derive from any clear, guiding basic concept and are therefore superficial and in part, even, obviously false. Virtues are qualities of will: wisdom belongs first and foremost to the intellect. *Sophrosune*, which Cicero translates as *temperantia* and which is in German *Mässigkeit* and in English *moderation*, is a very vague and ambiguous expression under which many different things can be subsumed, such as prudence, sobriety, keeping one's head. Bravery is not a virtue at all: though it is sometimes a servant or instrument of virtue, it is just as ready to serve the unworthiest ends: actually it is a temperamental quality. Even so early a writer as Geulinx[2] rejects the Platonic cardinal virtues (in his *Ethics*) and substitutes *diligentia, obedientia, justitia, humilitas* – an obviously bad selection. The Chinese name five cardinal virtues: pity, justice, politeness, wisdom and honesty (*Journal asiatique*, vol. 9) – Christianity has not cardinal but theological virtues: faith, hope and charity.

What distinguishes a moral virtue from a moral vice is whether the basic feeling towards others behind it is one of envy or one of pity: for every man bears these two diametrically opposed qualities within him, inasmuch as they arise from the comparison between his own condition and that of others which he cannot help making; one or other of these qualities will become his basic disposition and determine the nature of his actions according to the effect this comparison has on his individual character. Envy reinforces the wall between Thou and I: pity makes it thin and transparent; indeed, it sometimes tears the wall down altogether, whereupon the distinction between I and Not-I disappears.

2. Arnold Geulinx (1624–69), Flemish philosopher and follower of Descartes.

3

That *bravery* which was spoken of above – or more precisely *courage*, which is what lies behind it (for bravery is only courage in war) – deserves to be looked at more closely. The ancients included courage among the virtues, cowardice among the vices: this assessment does not accord with the Christian outlook, which is directed towards sufferance and benevolence and whose doctrine forbids all enmity and, properly speaking, even resistance; so that this assessment of courage and cowardice no longer obtains. We have nonetheless to admit that cowardice does not seem to us to be very consistent with a noble character, the reason being that it betrays a too great solicitude for one's own person. Courage however implies that one is willing to face a present evil so as to prevent a greater evil in the future, while cowardice does the reverse. Now the nature of *endurance* is similar to that ascribed to courage, for endurance consists precisely in the clear consciousness that there exist greater evils than those present at the moment but that in seeking to escape or prevent the latter one might call down the former. Courage would consequently be a kind of *endurance*; and, since it is endurance which gives us the capacity for self-denial and self-overcoming of any kind, courage too is, through it, at any rate related to virtue.

Yet the question can perhaps be considered from an even higher point of view. It might be possible to trace all fear of death back to a deficiency in that natural metaphysic by virtue of which man bears within him the certainty that he exists just as much in everyone else, indeed in everything else, as he does in his own person, whose death cannot therefore be of very much concern to him. Possession of this certainty would, on the other hand, be the origin of heroic courage, which would consequently have the same origin as the virtues of justice and philanthropy. This is, to be sure, to look at the matter from a very exalted standpoint: on the other hand, it is not otherwise easy to explain why cowardice should be considered contemptible, personal courage noble and sublime; since from any lower standpoint there seems to be no reason why a finite individual which is to itself all-in-all – is indeed itself the fundamental condition for the existence of the rest of the world – should not place the preservation of this self before all else. A wholly immanent, that is to say purely empirical, explanation based on the utility of courage would be inadequate.

4

Every good human quality is related to a bad one into which it threatens to pass over; and every bad quality is similarly related to a good one. The reason we so often misunderstand people is that when we first make their acquaintance we mistake their bad qualities for the related good ones, or vice versa: thus a prudent man will seem cowardly, a thrifty one avaricious; or a spendthrift will seem liberal, a boor frank and straightforward, an impudent fellow full of noble self-confidence, and so on.

5

Whoever lives among men will again and again be tempted to assume that moral wickedness and intellectual incapacity are closely connected and spring from one root. The impression that this is so arises merely because they are so often found together; and this can be explained by the very frequent occurrence of both, which means they often have to live together under the same roof. Not that it can be denied that they play into the hands of one another to their mutual advantage, which is why so many people present so very disagreeable an appearance and why the world is as it is. For want of understanding is favourable for making baseness, wickedness and falsity appear visibly, while cleverness knows better how to conceal them. And, on the other hand, how often perversity prevents a man from seeing truths that his reason is quite capable of grasping.

Yet let no one give himself airs. Just as everyone, even the greatest genius, is decidedly stupid and ignorant in some sphere or other of knowledge and thereby proclaims his kinship with the essentially perverse and absurd human race, so everyone bears within him something altogether morally bad, and even the finest, indeed noblest character will sometimes surprise us by revealing distinct traits of baseness, as though he was thereby seeking to own his kinship with the human race, in which every degree of vileness is to be discovered.

With all this, however, the difference between man and man is incalculably great, and many would be appalled if they could see others as they really are. – Oh for an Asmodeus[3] of morals who would let his minions see not only through roofs and walls but also through the veil of pretence, falsity, hypocrisy, lies and deception which extends over everything, so that they would know how little true honesty there is in the world and how often, even where one least suspects it, all the virtuous outworks merely conceal the fact that, secretly and in the innermost recess, dishonesty sits at the helm. For our civilized world is nothing but a great masquerade. You encounter knights, parsons, soldiers, doctors, lawyers, priests, philosophers and a thousand more: but they are not what they appear – they are merely masks behind which as a rule money-grubbers are hiding. One man puts on the mask of justice the better to attack his fellows; another, with the same object in view, chooses that of public good and patriotism; a third that of religion and purity of faith. Many have put on the mask of philosophy, philanthropy and the like for their various ends. Women have a narrower range to choose from: usually they employ the masks of modesty, coyness, simplicity and demureness. Then there are universal masks without any special character, as it were dominoes, which are therefore to be met with everywhere: among these are strict honesty, politeness, sincere sympathy and grinning affability. Usually, as I say, there is nothing but industrialists, businessmen and speculators concealed behind all these masks. In this respect the only honest class is that of the tradesmen, since they alone give themselves out for what they are:

3. An evil spirit or demon of Jewish mythology.

they go about without any mask on, and thus they stand low in the social order.

But there are more serious considerations involved and worse things to report. Man is at bottom a dreadful wild animal. We know this wild animal only in the tamed state called civilization and we are therefore shocked by occasional outbreaks of its true nature: but if and when the bolts and bars of the legal order once fall apart and anarchy supervenes it reveals itself for what it is. For enlightenment on this matter, though, you have no need to wait until that happens: there exist hundreds of reports, recent and less recent, which will suffice to convince you that man is in no way inferior to the tiger or the hyena in pitilessness and cruelty. A weighty contemporary example is provided by the reply received by the British Anti-Slavery Society from the American Anti-Slavery Society in answer to its inquiries about the treatment of slaves in the slave-owning states of the North American Union: *Slavery and the Internal Slave-Trade in the United States of North America.* This book constitutes one of the heaviest of all indictments against mankind. No one can read it without horror, and few will not be reduced to tears: for whatever the reader of it may have heard or imagined or dreamed of the unhappy condition of the slaves, indeed of human harshness and cruelty in general, will fade into insignificance when he reads how these devils in human form, these bigoted, church-going, Sabbath-keeping scoundrels, especially the Anglican parsons among them, treat their innocent black brothers whom force and injustice have delivered into their devilish clutches. This book, which consists of dry but authentic and documented reports, rouses one's human feelings to such a degree of indignation that one could preach a crusade for the subjugation and punishment of the slave-owning states of North America. They are a blot on mankind. – But we do not need to go to the New World for examples. In the year 1848 it came to light that in England a husband or wife, or both in collusion, had not *once* but a hundred times poisoned their children one after the other, or tortured them to death with hunger and neglect, merely for the insurance money from burial clubs; children were insured with several, in some cases as many as twenty, such clubs (see *The Times*, 20, 22 and 23 September 1848).

Reports of this sort belong, it is true, to the blackest pages of mankind's criminal record. But the source of them and of everything like them is the inner and inborn nature of man, in which the first and foremost quality is a colossal egoism ready and eager to overstep the bounds of justice. Does the admitted necessity for a so anxiously guarded European balance of power not already contain a confession that man is a beast of prey which will pounce upon a weaker neighbour as soon as he notices his existence? And is this fact not confirmed every day in ordinary life?

Gobineau (*Des races humaines*) [4] called man *l'animal méchant par excellence*, which people took very ill because they felt it was aimed at them. But Gobineau was right: for man is the only animal which causes pain to others with no other object than causing pain. The other animals do it in the cause of appeasing their hunger or in the rage of battle. No animal ever torments another for the sake of tormenting: but man does so, and it is this which constitutes the *diabolical* nature which is far worse than the merely bestial.

The worst trait in human nature, however, is *Schadenfreude,*[5] since it is closely related to cruelty, indeed differs from this only as theory differs from practice, but generally arises under circumstances in which pity ought to arise, which, as its antithesis, is the true source of all genuine justice and love of mankind. The antithesis of pity in another sense is *envy,* inasmuch as it is excited by an antithetical cause: that it is the antithesis of pity derives first and foremost from what causes it, and only as a consequence of this cause does it become the feeling of envy itself. Thus envy, although reprehensible, admits of some

4. Count Joseph Arthur de Gobineau (1816–82), orientalist and philosopher.
5. Untranslatable word meaning pleasure in another's discomfiture.

excuse and is humanly understandable, while *Schadenfreude* is diabolical and its derision is the laughter of Hell.

Now if, having taken stock of human *wickedness* as we have just done, you feel a sense of horror at it, you should straight-away turn your eyes to the *misery* of human existence. (And if you are shocked at its misery you should turn your eyes to its wickedness.) Then you will see that they balance one another; you will become aware of the existence of an eternal justice, that the world itself is its own universal Last Judgement, and you will begin to understand why everything that lives must atone for its existence, first by living and then by dying.

6

Readers of my ethical philosophy will know that with me the foundation of morality ultimately rests on the truth which is in the Veda and Vedanta expressed in the mystical formula *tat twam asi* (This art Thou), by which is meant every living thing, whether man or animal: it is called the *Mahavakya*, the great word.

The recognition of one's own essential being in another, objectively present individual is most clearly and beautifully evident in those cases in which a human being already on the brink of death is anxiously and actively concerned with the welfare and rescue of others. Of this kind is the well-known story of the servant girl who was one night bitten in the yard by a mad dog; believing herself beyond help, she seized the dog, dragged it to the kennel and locked the door, so that no one else should fall victim to it. Another example is the incident in Naples immortalized by Tischbein[6] in one of his water colours: a son bearing his aged father on his back is fleeing from a stream of lava which is rushing down towards the sea; when there remains only a narrow strip of land left between the two destruc-

6. Johann Friedrich August Tischbein (1751–1812), painter: he made portraits of many in Goethe's circle, and his best known work, 'Goethe in the Campagna', is also the best known portrait of Goethe.

tive elements, the father bids his son lay him down and save himself, since otherwise both will perish. The son obeys and in departing looks back at his father in a last farewell. This is what the painting depicts. Entirely apposite too is the historical event depicted by the masterly hand of Walter Scott in *The Heart of Midlothian* : two criminals have been condemned to death; one of them, whose ineptitude has led to the capture of of the other, overpowers the guard in the church after the funeral sermon and succeeds in freeing his companion without making any attempt to free himself. Also to be included here indeed – although the Western reader might find it offensive – is a scene often reproduced in copperplate print in which a soldier kneeling to be shot by a firing-squad is violently shooing away his dog, who is running up to him. – In every case of this kind we see an individual who is with perfect certainty going to meet his immediate destruction ceasing to think about his own preservation in order to direct all his attention and effort to that of another. What could possibly express more clearly the consciousness that this destruction is only the destruction of a phenomenon and is therefore itself phenomenon, while the essential being of him who faces destruction remains unaffected : it continues to exist in the other in whom at precisely this point he so clearly recognizes it, as his actions prove. For if this were not so; if we had before us a being actually about to be annihilated; how could this being betray so intense an interest in the welfare and continued existence of another as it does betray in expending its last energies to this end?

There are in fact two antithetical ways of becoming conscious of one's own existence : firstly, by empirical perception, by seeing it as it appears from without, an evanescently small existence in a world boundless in space and time, as one among the thousand million human beings who run around on this earth and do so for a very brief time, renewing themselves every thirty years; secondly, however, by plunging into one's own inner self and realizing that it is all-in-all and actually the only real being which, as an addition, sees itself reflected in its outward form as if in a mirror. That the former mode of knowledge comprehends merely phenomena conveyed through the agency of the *principium individuationis*, but the latter is a direct perception of one's being as thing in itself – this is a theory in which I am supported as regards the first part by Kant, but as regards both parts by the Veda. The simple objection to the latter mode of knowledge is, of course, that it presupposes that one and the same being can be at different places at the same time and yet be wholly present in each of them. But if this is from the empirical standpoint a palpable impossibility, indeed an absurdity, it is nonetheless perfectly true of the thing in itself, because that impossibility and absurdity depends entirely on the phenomenal forms which constitute the *principium individuationis*. For the thing in itself, the will to live, is present whole and undivided in every single being, even the most insignificant, as completely as in all that have ever been, are or will be, taken together. And in truth, if every other being were to perish, the entire being in itself of the world would still exist unharmed and undiminished in this single one remaining and would laugh at the destruction of all the rest as an illusion. This is, to be sure, a conclusion *per impossibile*, to which one is quite entitled to oppose this other, that if any being whatever, even the most insignificant, were to be utterly annihilated, the whole world would perish in and with it. It is in precisely this sense that the mystic Angelus Silesius says:

> Ich weiss, dass ohne mich Gott nicht ein Nu kann leben:
> Werd' ich zunicht; er muss von Noth den Geist aufgeben.[7]

7

After my prize essay on moral freedom[8] no thinking person can remain in any doubt that moral freedom is never to be sought in nature but only outside of nature. It is metaphysical;

7. I know that without me God cannot live for an instant: if I perish he must needs give up the ghost. Angelus Silesius is the adopted name of Johannes Scheffler (1624–77), mystical poet.

8. 'Ueber die Freiheit des menschlichen Willens', published in 1841 in *Die beiden Grundprobleme der Ethik*.

in the physical world it is impossible. Our individual actions are, consequently, in no way free; on the other hand, the individual character of each of us must be regarded as a free act. It is as it is because it wants, once and for all, to be as it is. For will itself and in itself – even when it appears as an individual and thus constitutes the individual's original and fundamental volition – is independent of all knowledge, because it precedes all knowledge. What it receives from knowledge is merely the motivations by which its nature evolves in successive stages and makes itself distinguishable or visible: but will itself, since it lies outside of time, is unchangeable for as long as it exists at all. So that every individual, as he once and for all is, and under the circumstances obtaining at any particular moment – which for their part are governed by strict necessity – can absolutely never do anything other than precisely what he does at that particular moment. Consequently the entire empirical course of a man's life is, in great things and in small, as necessarily predetermined as clockwork. The fundamental reason this is so is that the mode in which the metaphysical free act referred to enters the knowing consciousness is that of perception, the form of which is space and time; through the agency of space and time the unity and indivisibility of this act from then on appears drawn out into a series of states and occurrences which take place in accordance with the principle of sufficient reason in its four forms, this being precisely what is meant by *necessity*. The outcome however is a moral one, namely this, that by what we do we know what we are, just as by what we suffer we know what we deserve.

8

The question has been raised what two men who have grown up entirely alone in the desert would do when they met one another for the first time. Hobbes, Pufendorf and Rousseau have given quite different answers to this question.[9] Pufendorf

9. Thomas Hobbes (1588–1679), one of the greatest British philosophers; Samuel Pufendorf (1632–94), German jurist and philosopher; Jean-Jacques Rousseau (1712–78), the most influential French philosopher.

believed they would approach one another affectionately; Hobbes, that they would be hostile; Rousseau, that they would pass one another by in silence. All three are both right and wrong: the *immeasurable difference between the inborn moral disposition of one individual and another* would in precisely this situation reveal itself in so clear a light that such a meeting would be, as it were, a standard of measurement of this disposition. In some men the sight of other men at once arouses a hostile feeling, in that their inmost being declares: 'Not me!' There are others in whom it at once arouses a friendly interest: their inmost being says: 'Me once more!' Countless gradations lie between these two extremes. – But that we differ so fundamentally on this cardinal point is a great problem, indeed a mystery.

9

It is a wonderful thing how the *individuality* of *every* man (i.e. a certain particular character with a certain particular intellect) minutely determines his every thought and action and like a penetrative dye permeates even the most insignificant part of them, so that the entire life-course, i.e. the inner and outer history, of each one differs fundamentally from that of all the others. As a botanist can recognize the whole plant from one leaf, as Cuvier [10] can construct the whole animal from one bone, so an accurate knowledge of a man's character can be arrived at from a single characteristic action; and that is true even when this action involves some trifle – indeed this is often better for the purpose, for with important things people are on their guard, while with trifles they follow their own nature without much reflection.

The true basis and propaedeutic for all knowledge of human nature is the persuasion that a man's actions are, essentially and as a whole, not directed by his reason and its designs; so that no one becomes this or that because he wants to, though he

10. Georges Léopold Chrétien Frédéric Dagobert, Baron Cuvier (1769–1832), naturalist.

want to never so much, but that his conduct proceeds from his inborn and inalterable character, is more narrowly and in particulars determined by motivation, and is thus necessarily the product of these two factors.

If you grasp this you will also see that we can really never make more than a supposition about what we will do in any future situation, although we often think we have made a decision about it. If, e.g., a man undertakes to do this or that should certain circumstances arise in the future, and gives this undertaking with the firmest intention of carrying it out, even with the liveliest desire to carry it out, this does not by any means ensure that he *will* carry it out, unless he is so constituted that his given promise itself and as such becomes a constantly sufficient motivation, so that with regard to his honour it operates on him like an external compulsion. What he will actually do when these circumstances arise can, moreover, be predicted only from a true and perfect knowledge of his character and of the external circumstances under whose influence he has then come; although if these conditions were met, it could be predicted with absolute certainty. The unalterability of our character and the necessary nature of our actions will be brought home with uncommon force to anyone who has on any occasion behaved as he ought not to have behaved, who has been lacking in resolution or constancy or courage or some other quality demanded by the circumstances of the moment. Afterwards he honestly recognizes and regrets his failing, and no doubt thinks: 'I'll do better another time.' Another time comes, the circumstances are repeated, and he does as he did before – to his great astonishment.

The best illustration of the truth here under discussion is provided in general by the plays of Shakespeare. For he was thoroughly convinced of it and his intuitive wisdom expresses itself *in concreto* on all sides. I would like to exemplify it, however, with a case in which he emphasizes it with particular clarity: I mean the character of the Earl of Northumberland, whom we see traverse three tragedies without ever really taking a major role in the drama but, on the contrary, appearing in only a few scenes spread over fifteen acts; so that unless you give it all your attention you can easily lose sight of the moral consistency of his character, though the poet never lost sight of it. Whenever Northumberland appears Shakespeare allows him a noble, knightly demeanour and gives him language appropriate to it – indeed, he sometimes has very beautiful and even sublime passages to speak, since Shakespeare's practice is very far removed from that of Schiller, who likes to paint the Devil black and whose moral approval or disapproval of the characters he is drawing is audible in the words they themselves speak. In the case of Shakespeare, as also in that of Goethe, every character is, while he stands and speaks, entirely in the right, though he be the Devil himself. Compare in this respect Goethe's Duke of Alba with Schiller's.[11] We first make the acquaintance of the Earl of Northumberland in *Richard II*, where he is the first to plot against the king in favour of Bolingbroke, later Henry IV, whom he has earlier (Act III, scene 3) personally flattered. In the following act he is reproved for referring to the king simply as Richard, which however he asserts he did merely for the sake of brevity. Soon afterwards it is his insidious speech which persuades the king to capitulate. In the following act, in the scene in which he abdicates, Northumberland treats him with such disdain and harshness that the unhappy broken monarch for once loses his patience and cries: 'Fiend, thou torment'st me ere I come to hell!' At the end of the play he informs the new king that he has sent the severed heads of his predecessor's followers to London. – In the following tragedy, *Henry IV*, he plots against the new king in the same way as he did against the old. In the fourth act we see the rebels joined together preparing for the following day's decisive battle and impatiently awaiting the arrival only of him and his forces. At length a letter arrives from him: he himself is sick but he cannot entrust his forces to another; nonetheless, they should courageously proceed with the business and go bravely to battle. This they do: but, decidedly weakened by his absence, they are totally defeated, most of their leaders are

11. In Goethe's *Egmont* and Schiller's *Don Carlos*.

captured, and Northumberland's own son, the valiant Hotspur, falls at the hands of the Crown Prince. – We see him again in the following play, the second part of *Henry IV*, where he is wild with rage at the death of his son and breathing the most fearful vengeance, in pursuit of which he incites renewed rebellion. Its leaders again assemble; as they are preparing, in the fourth act, to give the decisive battle and are waiting only for him to join them, a letter arrives: he has been unable to collect together a sufficient force, so he intends for the present to seek safety in Scotland; nonetheless, he sincerely wishes them every success in their valiant undertaking. Whereupon they surrender to the king under a pact which the king fails to honour, and thus perish.

The Fate of the ancients is nothing other than the conscious certainty that all events are bound firmly together by the chain of causality and thus occur with strict necessity, so that the future is already totally fixed and precisely determined, and can no more be altered than the past can.

I

IF you start from the preconceived opinion that the concept of *justice* must be a *positive* concept and then undertake to define it, you won't get very far: you will be trying to embrace a shadow, pursuing a ghost, looking for a *nonens*. For the concept of *justice* is, like that of *freedom*, a *negative* concept: its content is a pure negation. The concept of *injustice* is the positive one, and means the same thing as *injury* in the broadest sense, that is to say *laesio*. Such an injury may affect the person or property or honour. – It is accordingly easy to define *human rights*: everyone has the right to do anything that does not injure another.

To have a right *to* something means no more than to be able to do it, or take it, or use it without thereby injuring anyone. – This exposes the meaninglessness of many questions, e.g. whether we have the right to take our own life: for so far as any claims others can have upon us are concerned, these are conditional upon our being alive and lapse when this condition lapses. That anyone who no longer wishes to live for himself must go on living merely as a machine for others to use is an extravagant demand.

2

Although men possess unequal powers, they nonetheless possess equal rights. Rights are not based on powers: because of the moral nature of justice, they are based on the fact that in each man the same will to live appears at the same stage of its objectivization. Yet this is valid only in respect of original and abstract rights, which man possesses as man. The property, likewise the honour which each man has acquired by means of his powers are in accordance with the measure and the nature of these powers and then extend the sphere of his rights: it is here that equality therefore ceases. He who is better endowed or more active in this respect extends through his greater acquisitions, not his rights, but only the number of things to which they extend.

3

I have shown in my chief work (Volume II, chapter 47)[1] that the *state* is essentially no more than an institution for the protection of the whole against attacks from without and the protection of its individual members from attacks by one another. It follows that the necessity for the state ultimately depends on the acknowledged *injustice* of the human race: without this no one would ever have thought of the state, since no one would have needed to fear any encroachment on his rights, and a mere union against the attacks of wild animals or the elements would bear only a very slight similarity to a state. From this point of view it is easy to see the ignorance and triviality of those philosophasters who, in pompous phrases, represent the state as the supreme goal and greatest achievement of mankind and thereby achieve an apotheosis of philistinism.

4

If *justice* ruled on earth it would be sufficient to have *built* one's house: it would require no further protection than this manifest right of possession. But because *injustice* is the order of the day, whoever built the house must also be in a position to protect it, otherwise his right is *de facto* defective: for the assailant has on his side *force majeure*, which is actually Spinoza's concept of justice: he recognizes no other right, but says: *'Unusquisque tantum juris habet, quantum potentiâ valet'* and *'Uniuscujusque jus potentiâ ejus definitur'*.[2] In civil life, to be sure, this concept

1. *The World as Will and Idea* is meant.
2. A person's rights are equivalent to his power (*Tractatus Politicus* 2, 8). The rights of a person are determined by his power (*Ethics* IV, 37, note 1).

of justice has been abolished in practice as well as in theory; but in political life it has been abolished only in theory: in practice it continues to prevail.

5

The difference between serfdom, as in Russia, and landed property, as in England, and that between the serf and the tenant, occupier, mortgagor, etc., in general, lies more in the form than the content. It makes little essential difference to me whether I own the peasant or the land he works, the bird or its food, the fruit or the tree: as Shylock says:

> you take my life
> When you do take the means whereby I live.[3]

The free peasant has, of course, the advantage that he can leave and go off into the wide world; but the serf has this perhaps greater advantage that when there is a bad harvest, or when he is sick or old or incapable, his master has to take care of him.

Poverty and slavery are thus only two forms of – one might almost say two words for – the same thing, the essence of which is that a man's energies are expended for the most part not on his own behalf but on that of others; the outcome being partly that he is overloaded with work, partly that his needs are very inadequately met.

6

The question of the sovereignty of the people amounts at bottom to the question whether anyone could have the natural right to rule a people against its will. I cannot see how that question could be answered affirmatively. It is therefore a fact that the people is sovereign: but this sovereignty never comes of age and therefore has to remain under the permanent care of a guardian: it can never exercise its rights itself without giving

3. *The Merchant of Venice*, Act IV, scene 1.

rise to limitless dangers, especially as, like all minors, it is easily fooled by cunning imposters, who are therefore called demagogues.

Voltaire says: *'Le premier qui fut roi fut un soldat heureux.'*[4] All princes were no doubt in fact originally victorious commanders, and for a long time ruled as such. Having acquired standing armies, they regarded the people as a means of feeding themselves and their soldiers, that is to say as a herd which one looks after so that it may provide wool, milk and meat. This is based on the fact that, by nature and from the first, it is not *justice* which rules on earth but *force* (as will be more fully discussed in the following section); force has the advantage of the *primus occupans*, which is why it can never be annulled or really abolished from the world: it must always be appealed to, and the most that one can hope for is that it will stand on the side of justice. Consequently, what the prince says is: I rule over you by force: to do that I must exclude every other force, for I will not suffer any other force to stand beside mine, neither that which comes from without, nor that of one against another within: so learn to be content with force. It is precisely because this claim was made good that in time something quite different evolved out of kingship, and the old conception of it stepped into the background. It was replaced by the conception of a national father, and the king became the firm unshakeable pillar on which alone the entire legal order and thus the rights of all repose and continue to exist. But he can perform this role only by virtue of the *inborn* prerogative which bestows upon him and only him an authority above every other which cannot be doubted or contested and which, indeed, everyone obeys as if by instinct. Thus he is rightly called 'by the grace of God', and is at all times the most useful person in the state, whose services cannot be rewarded too highly by any civil list, no matter how costly.

4. The first king was a successful soldier.

7

Justice is in itself powerless: what rules by nature is *force*. To draw this over on to the side of justice, so that by means of force justice rules – that is the problem of statecraft, and it is certainly a hard one: how hard you will realize if you consider what boundless egoism reposes in almost every human breast; and that it is many millions of individuals so constituted who have to be kept within the bounds of peace, order and legality. This being so, it is a wonder the world is on the whole as peaceful and law-abiding as we see it to be – which situation, however, is brought about only by the machinery of the state. For the only thing that can produce an immediate effect is physical force, since this is the only thing which men as they generally are understand and respect.

Freedom of the press is to the machinery of the state what the safety-valve is to the steam engine: every discontent is by means of it immediately relieved in words – indeed, unless this discontent is very considerable, it exhausts itself in this way. If, however, it *is* very considerable, it is as well to know of it in time, so as to redress it. – On the other hand, however, freedom of the press must be regarded as a permit to sell poison: poison of the mind and poison of the heart. For what cannot be put into the heads of the ignorant and credulous masses? – especially if you hold before them the prospect of gain and advantages. And of what misdeeds is man not capable once something has been put into his head? I very much fear, therefore, that the dangers of press freedom outweigh its usefulness, especially where there are legal remedies available for all grievances. In any event, however, freedom of the press should be conditional upon the strictest prohibition of any kind of anonymity.

A constitution embodying nothing but abstract justice would be a wonderful thing, but it would not be suited to beings such as men. Because the great majority of men are in the highest degree egoistic, unjust, inconsiderate, deceitful, sometimes even malicious, and equipped moreover with very mediocre intelligence, there exists the need for a completely unaccountable power, concentrated in one man and standing above even justice and the law, before which everything bows and which is regarded as a being of a higher order, a sovereign by the grace of God. Only thus can mankind in the long run be curbed and ruled.

The monarchical form of government is the form most natural to man. How could it possibly happen that, universally and at all times, many millions, even hundreds of millions, of us men have subjected ourselves to and willingly obeyed one man, occasionally even a woman or, provisionally, a child, if there were not in man a monarchical instinct which drives him to it as to the condition most appropriate to him? For this does not proceed from reflection. Everywhere one man is king, and his dignity is, as a rule, hereditary. He is, as it were, the personification or monogram of the whole people, which in him acquires individuality: in this sense he can justly say: *l'état c'est moi*. It is for precisely this reason that in Shakespeare's histories the kings of England and France refer to one another as 'England' and 'France' and the duke of Austria (in *King John*) is referred to as 'Austria': it is as though they regarded themselves as incarnations of their nationalities. This is in accord with human nature, and is precisely why the hereditary monarch cannot divorce his own and his family's welfare from that of his country, which is what elected monarchs usually do – as witness the Papal States. – Republics are anti-natural, artificial and derive from reflection: consequently there are also very few of them in the entire history of mankind, namely the little Greek republics and the Roman and Carthaginian republics, and these were all made possible by the fact that five-sixths, perhaps even seven-eighths of their population consisted of *slaves*. The case is similar in the United States of North America: in the year 1840, of a population of 16 millions, three millions were slaves. The duration of the republics of antiquity was, moreover, very brief compared with that of the monarchies. – Republics are in general easy to establish but hard to maintain: precisely the opposite is true of monarchies.

If you want Utopian plans, I would say: the only solution to the problem is the despotism of the wise and noble members of a genuine aristocracy, a genuine nobility, achieved by mating the most magnanimous men with the cleverest and most gifted women. This proposal constitutes *My Utopia* and my Platonic Republic.

8

People have always been very discontented with governments, laws and public institutions; for the most part, however, this has been only because they have been ready to blame them for the wretchedness which pertains to human existence as such. But this misrepresentation has never been put forward in more deceitful and impudent a fashion than it is by the demagogues of the present day. As enemies of Christianity, they are optimists: and according to them the world is 'an end in itself', and thus in its natural constitution an altogether splendid structure, a regular abode of bliss. The colossal evil of the world which cries against this idea they attribute entirely to governments: if these would only do their duty there would be Heaven on earth, i.e. we could all, without work or effort, cram ourselves, swill, propagate and drop dead – for this is a paraphrase of their 'end in itself' and the goal of the 'unending progress of mankind' which in pompous phrases they never weary of proclaiming.

ON AESTHETICS

I

THE intrinsic problem of the metaphysics of the beautiful can be stated very simply: how is it possible for us to take pleasure in an object when this object has no kind of connexion with our desires?

For we all feel that pleasure in a thing can really arise only from its relation to our will or, as we like to put it, our aims; so that pleasure divorced from a stimulation of the will seems to be a contradiction. Yet it is quite obvious that the beautiful as such excites pleasure in us without having any kind of connexion with our personal aims, that is to say with our will.

My solution to this problem has been that in the beautiful we always perceive the intrinsic and primary forms of animate and inanimate nature, that is to say Plato's Ideas thereof, and that this perception stipulates the existence of its essential correlative, the *will-less subject of knowledge*, i.e. a pure intelligence without aims or intentions. Through this, when an aesthetic perception occurs the will completely vanishes from consciousness. But will is the sole source of all our troubles and sufferings. This is the origin of the feeling of pleasure which accompanies the perception of the beautiful. It therefore rests on the abolition of all possibility of suffering. – If it should be objected that the possibility of pleasure would then also be abolished, one should remember that, as I have often demonstrated, happiness, gratification, is of a *negative* nature, namely the mere cessation of suffering, pain on the other hand positive. Thus, when all desire disappears from consciousness there still remains the condition of pleasure, i.e. the absence of all pain, and in this case the absence even of the possibility of pain, in that the individual is transformed from a willing subject into a purely knowing subject, yet continues to be conscious of himself and of his actions as a knowing subject. As we know, the world as *will* is the primary (*ordine prior*) and the world as *idea* the secondary world (*ordine posterior*). The former is the world of desire and consequently that of pain and thousandfold misery. The latter, however, is in itself intrinsically painless: in addition it contains a remarkable spectacle, altogether significant or at the very least entertaining. Enjoyment of this spectacle constitutes aesthetic pleasure.

2

If, however, the individual will sets its associated power of imagination free for a while, and for once releases it entirely from the service for which it was made and exists, so that it abandons the tending of the will or of the individual person which alone is its natural theme and thus its regular occupation, and yet does not cease to be energetically active or to extend to their fullest extent its powers of perceptivity, then it will forthwith become completely *objective*, i.e. it will become a faithful mirror of objects, or more precisely the medium of the objectivization of the will appearing in this or that object, the inmost nature of which will now come forth through it the more completely the longer perception lasts, until it has been entirely exhausted. It is only thus, with the pure subject, that there arises the pure object, i.e. the complete manifestation of the will appearing in the object perceived, which is precisely the (Platonic) *Idea* of it. The perception of this, however, demands that, when contemplating an object, I really abstract its position in space and time, and thus abstract its individuality. For it is this *position*, always determined by the law of causality, which places this object in any kind of relationship to me as an individual; so that only when this position is done away with will the object become an *Idea* and I therewith a pure subject of knowledge. This is why a painting, by fixing for ever the fleeting moment and thus extricating it from time, presents not the individual but the *Idea*, the enduring element in all change. But this postulated change in subject and object requires not only that the faculty of knowledge be released from its original servitude and given over entirely to itself, but also that it should remain active to the full extent of its capacity, notwithstanding that the natural spur to its activity, the instigation of the will, is now lacking. Here is where the difficulty and thus the rarity of the thing lies; because all our thought and endeavour, all our hearing and seeing, stand by nature directly or indirectly in the service of our countless personal aims, big and small, and consequently it is the *will* which spurs on the faculty of knowledge to the fulfilment of its functions, without which instigation it immediately weakens. Moreover, knowledge activated by this instigation completely suffices for practical life, even for the various branches of science, since they direct themselves to the *relations* between things and not to their intrinsic and inner being. Wherever it is a question of knowledge of cause and effect or of grounds and consequences of any kind, that is to say in all branches of natural science and mathematics, as also in history, or with inventions, etc., the knowledge sought must be an *aim of the will*, and the more vehemently it strives for it, the sooner it will be attained. Likewise in affairs of state, in war, in finance and business, in intrigues of every sort, and so on, the *will* must first of all, through the vehemence of its desire, compel the intellect to exert all its energies so as to track down all the reasons and consequences of the affair in question. Indeed, it is astonishing how far beyond the normal measure of its energies the spur of the will can drive a given intellect in such a case.

The situation is quite different with the perception of the objective, intrinsic being of things which constitutes their (Platonic) Idea and which must lie behind every achievement in the fine arts. For the will, which in the former case promoted the endeavour and was indeed indispensable to it, must here take no part whatever: for here only that serves which the intellect achieves quite alone and by its own means and presents as a voluntary gift. For only in the condition of *pure knowledge*, where will and its aims have been completely removed from man, but with them his individuality also, can that purely objective perception arise in which the (Platonic)

Ideas of things will be comprehended. But such a perception must always precede the conception, i.e. the first, intuitive knowledge which afterwards constitutes the intrinsic material and kernel, as it were the soul of an authentic work of art or poem, or indeed of a genuine philosophy. The unpremeditated, unintentional, indeed in part unconscious and instinctive element which has always been remarked in works of *genius* owes its origin to precisely the fact that primal artistic knowledge is entirely separated from and independent of will, is will-less.

3

As for the *objective* aspect of this aesthetic perception, that is to say the (Platonic) Idea, it may be described as that which we would have before us if time, the formal and subjective condition of our knowledge, were drawn away, like the glass lens from a kaleidoscope. We see, e.g., the development of bud, flower and fruit and marvel at the driving force which never wearies of producing this series again and again. Our amazement would cease if we could know that with all this changing development we have before us only the one, unchangeable Idea of the plant, which however we are incapable of perceiving as a unity of bud, flower and fruit, but are compelled to apprehend under the form of time through which the Idea is displayed to our intellect in these successive states.

4

If you consider how poetry and the plastic arts always take an *individual* for their theme and present it with the most careful exactitude in all its uniqueness, down to the most insignificant characteristics; and if you then look at the sciences, which operate by means of *concepts* each of which represents countless individuals by once and for all defining and designating what is peculiar to them as a species; – if you consider this, the practice of art is likely to seem to you paltry, petty and indeed almost childish. The nature of art, however, is such that in art one single case stands for thousands, in that what art has in view with that careful and particular delineation of the individual is the revelation of the *Idea* of the genus to which it belongs; so that, e.g., an occurrence, a scene from human life depicted correctly and completely, that is to say with an exact delineation of the individuals involved in it, leads to a clear and profound knowledge of the Idea of humanity itself perceived from this or that aspect. For as the botanist plucks one single flower from the endless abundance of the plant world and then analyses it so as to demonstrate to us the nature of the plant in general, so the poet selects a single scene, indeed sometimes no more than a single mood or sensation, from the endless confusion of ceaselessly active human life, in order to show us what the life and nature of man is. This is why we see the greatest spirits – Shakespeare and Goethe, Raphael and Rembrandt – not disdaining to delineate single individuals, and not even notable ones, and to make them visible before us, and doing so with the greatest exactitude and the most earnest application, in their whole particularity down to the very smallest details. For the particular and individual can be grasped only when it is made visible – which is why I have defined poetry as the art of setting the imagination into action by means of words.

5

A work of plastic art does not show us, as actuality does, that which exists once and never again, namely the union of this particular material with this particular form which constitutes the concrete and individual; it shows us *the form* alone which, if it were presented completely and in all its aspects, would be the Idea itself. The picture therefore immediately leads us away from the individual to the pure form. The separation of form from material is already a big step towards the Idea: but every picture, whether a painting or a statue, constitutes such a separation. Now it is precisely because the aim of the aesthetic work of art is to bring us to a knowledge of the (Platonic) Idea that it is characterized by this separation, this dividing of the form from the material. It is *intrinsic* to the work of art to present the form alone, without the material, and to do so manifestly and obviously. This is really the reason waxwork figures make no aesthetic impression and are consequently not works of art (in the aesthetic sense), although when they are well made they produce a far greater illusion of reality than the best picture or statue can and if imitation of the actual were the aim of art would have to be accorded the first rank. For they seem to present not the pure form but with it the material as well, so that they bring about the illusion that the thing itself is standing there. The true work of art leads us from that which exists only once and never again, i.e. the individual, to that which exists perpetually and time and time again in innumerable manifestations, the pure form or Idea; but the waxwork figure appears to present the individual itself, that is to say that which exists only once and never again, but without that which lends value to such a fleeting existence, without life. That is why the waxwork evokes a feeling of horror: it produces the effect of a rigid corpse.

6

The reason the impressions we receive in youth are so significant, the reason why in the dawn of life everything appears to us in so ideal and transfigured a light, is that we then first become acquainted with the genus, which is still new to us, through the individual, so that every individual thing stands as a representative of its genus: we grasp therein the (Platonic) *Idea* of this genus, which is essentially what constitutes beauty.

7

The beauty and grace of the human figure united together are the will in its most clearly visible form at the highest stage of its objectivization, and this is why they are the supreme achievement of the plastic arts. On the other hand, every material thing is beautiful, consequently every animal is beautiful. If this is not evident to us in the case of certain animals it is because we are not in a position to regard them purely objectively and thus comprehend the Idea of them, but are prevented from doing so by some inescapable thought-association, usually the result of an obtrusive similarity, e.g. that of the ape to man, as a consequence of which instead of grasping the Idea of this animal we see only the caricature of a man. The similarity between the toad and mud and dirt seems to produce the same effect, although this is inadequate to explain the boundless repugnance, indeed terror and horror, which overcomes many people at the sight of this animal, as it does others in the case of the spider: this seems rather to originate in a much deeper, metaphysical and mysterious connexion.

8

Inorganic nature, provided it does not consist of water, produces a very melancholy, indeed oppressive impression upon us when it appears without anything organic. An instance is provided by the regions of bare rock without any vegetation in the long valley near Toulon through which runs the road to Marseille; but the deserts of Africa offer a much more grandiose and impressive example. The sadness of this impression produced upon us by the inorganic derives first and foremost from the fact that the inorganic mass is subject exclusively to the law of gravity, the direction of which consequently dictates everything. – On the other hand, we derive a high degree of immediate pleasure from the sight of vegetation, but this is naturally the greater the more abundant, manifold and extensive – that is to say left to itself – the vegetation is. The immediate reason for this lies in the fact that in vegetation the law of gravity seems to have been overcome, in that the plant world raises itself in precisely the opposite direction from the one dictated by this law and thus directly proclaims the phenomenon of life as a new and higher order of things. We ourselves are part of this order: it is that in nature which is related to us, the element of our existence. Our heart is uplifted in presence of it. What pleases us first and foremost at the sight of the plant world, therefore, is this vertical upward direction, and a group of trees gains vastly from having a couple of straight-rising pointed fir-trees in its midst. On the other hand, a felled tree no longer affects us; indeed, one that has grown up slanting already produces far less effect than an upright one; and it is the down-hanging branches of the weeping willow which have surrendered to gravity that have given this tree its name. – The melancholy effect of the inorganic nature of water is in large part abolished by its great mobility, which produces an impression of life, and by its constant play with light: it is, moreover, the primal condition of our life.

9

A man who tries to live on the generosity of the Muses, I mean on his poetic gifts, seems to me somewhat to resemble a girl who lives on her charms. Both profane for base profit what ought to be the free gift of their inmost being. Both are liable to become exhausted and both usually come to a shameful end. So do not degrade your Muse to a whore.

10

Music is the true universal language which is understood everywhere, so that it is ceaselessly spoken in all countries and throughout all the centuries with great zeal and earnestness, and a significant melody which says a great deal soon makes its way round the entire earth, while one poor in meaning which says nothing straightaway fades and dies: which proves that the content of a melody is very well understandable. Yet music speaks not of things but of pure weal and woe, which are the only realities for the *will*: that is why it speaks so much to the heart, while it has nothing to say *directly* to the head and it is a misuse of it to demand that it should do so, as happens in all *pictorial* music, which is consequently once and for all objectionable, even though Haydn and Beethoven strayed into composing it: Mozart and Rossini, so far as I know, never did. For expression of the passions is one thing, depiction of things another.

II

Grand opera is not really a product of the pure artistic sense, it is rather the somewhat barbaric conception of enhancing aesthetic enjoyment by piling up the means to it, by the simultaneous production of quite disparate impressions and by strengthening the effect through augmenting the masses and forces producing it; while music, as the mightiest of the arts, is capable by itself of completely engrossing the mind receptive to it; indeed, its highest products, if they are to be properly comprehended and enjoyed, demand the undivided and undistracted attention of the entire mind, so that it may surrender to them and immerse itself in them in order to understand their incredibly intimate language. Instead of which, the mind is invaded through the eye, while listening to a highly complex piece of operatic music, by the most colourful pageantry, the most fanciful pictures and the liveliest impressions of light and colour; and at the same time it is occupied with the plot of the action. Through all this it is distracted and confused and its attention is diverted, so that it is very little receptive to the sacred, mysterious, intimate language of music. All these accompaniments are thus diametrically opposed to the attainment of the musical aim.

Strictly speaking one could call opera an unmusical invention for the benefit of unmusical minds, in as much as music first has to be smuggled in through a medium foreign to it, for instance as the accompaniment to a long drawn out, insipid love story and its poetic pap: for a spirited compact poem full of matter is of no use as an opera text, because the composition cannot be equal to such a poem.

The mass and the symphony alone provide undisturbed, fully musical enjoyment, while in opera the music is miserably involved with the vapid drama and its mock poetry and must try to bear the foreign burden laid on it as best it can. The mocking contempt with which the great Rossini sometimes handles the text is, while not exactly praiseworthy, at any rate genuinely musical.

In general, however, grand opera, by more and more deadening our musical receptivity through its three-hours duration and at the same time putting our patience to the test through the snail's pace of what is usually a very trite action, is in itself intrinsically and essentially boring; which failing can be overcome only by the excessive excellence of an individual achievement: that is why in this genre only the masterpieces are enjoyable and everything mediocre is unendurable.

12

Drama in general, as the most perfect reflection of human existence, has three modes of comprehending it. At the first and most frequently encountered stage it remains at what is merely interesting: we are involved with the characters because they pursue their own designs, which are similar to our own; the action goes forward by means of intrigue, the nature of the characters, and chance; wit and humour season the whole. – At the second stage drama becomes sentimental: pity is aroused for the hero, and through him for ourselves; the action is characterized by pathos, yet at the end it comes back to peace and contentment. – At the highest and hardest stage the *tragic* is aimed at: grievous suffering, the misery of existence is brought before us, and the final outcome is here the vanity of all human striving. We are deeply affected and the sensation of the will's turning away from life is aroused in us, either directly or as a simultaneously sounding harmony.

13

The first step is the hardest – says the popular adage. But in dramaturgy the reverse is true: the last step is the hardest. Evidence of this is the countless dramas the first half of which promises well but which then become confused, halt, waver, especially in the notorious fourth act, and finally come to a forced or unsatisfying end, or to one everybody has long since foreseen; sometimes, as with *Emilia Galotti*,[1] the end is even revolting and sends the audience home in a thoroughly bad mood. This difficulty of the *dénouement* is the result partly of the fact that it is easier to confuse things than to straighten them out again, but partly too of the fact that at the beginning of the play we allow the dramatist *carte blanche*, while at the end we make certain definite demands of him. We demand that the outcome shall be a completely happy or a completely tragic one – but it is not easy to make human affairs take so definite a direction. We then demand that this outcome shall be achieved naturally, fairly and in an unforced way – and yet at the same time not have been foreseen by the audience.

A *novel* will be the higher and nobler the more *inner* and less *outer* life it depicts; and this relation will accompany every grade of novel as its characteristic sign, from *Tristram Shandy* down to the crudest and most action-packed romance. *Tristram Shandy*, to be sure, has as good as no action whatever; but how very little action there is in *La Nouvelle Héloïse* and *Wilhelm Meister!*[2] Even *Don Quixote* has relatively little, and what there is is very trivial, amounting to no more than a series of jokes. And these four novels are the crown of the genre. Consider, further, the marvellous novels of Jean Paul and see how much inner life is set in motion on the narrowest of external foundations. Even the novels of Walter Scott have a significant preponderance of inner over outer life, and the latter appears only with a view to setting the former in motion; while in bad novels the outer action is there for its own sake. The art lies in setting the inner life into the most violent motion with the smallest possible expenditure of outer life: for it is the inner life which is the real object of our interest. – The task of the novelist is not to narrate great events but to make small ones interesting.

1. Tragedy by Gotthold Ephraim Lessing (1729–81), a leader of the Enlightenment in Germany and the principal German dramatist before the age of Goethe and Schiller.

2. *La Nouvelle Héloïse* is by Rousseau, *Wilhelm Meister* by Goethe.

ON PSYCHOLOGY

I

THE *will* to live, which constitutes the inmost kernel of every living thing, appears most unconcealedly in the higher, that is to say cleverest animals, and its nature may in them consequently be observed most plainly. *Beneath* this stage it does not appear so clearly, has a lower degree of objectivization; *above* it, however – that is to say, in man – the presence of reason means the existence of circumspection, and with it the capacity for dissimulation, which straightway throws a veil over the will. Here the will therefore steps out unconcealed only in outbursts of emotion and passion: and this is why when passion speaks it always, and rightly, inspires belief, no matter what passion it may be. It is for the same reason that the passions are the principal theme of the poets and the actors' showpiece. – It is on the previously mentioned fact, however, that our pleasure in dogs, monkeys, cats, etc., depends: it is the perfect *naïveté* of all their actions which so delights us.

2

Many things attributed to *force of habit* depend rather on the constancy and unalterability of our primary and inborn character, in consequence of which under similar circumstances we always do the *same* thing, with the same necessity the hundredth time as the first time. – Genuine *force of habit*, on the other hand, really derives from the *inertia* which wants to spare the intellect and the will the labour, difficulty and sometimes the danger involved in making a fresh choice, and which therefore lets us do today what we did yesterday and a hundred times before that, and what we know will meet the case.

The truth of the matter, however, lies deeper: for it is to be understood in a more particular sense than seems to be the case at first sight. That which is to the body in so far as it is activated by purely mechanical causes the *force of inertia*, is to the body which is moved by motivations the *force of habit*. The actions we perform out of pure habit really occur without any individual, special motivation, which is why we do not really think about them while we are performing them. Only the first instance of any action which has become a habit was motivated: the secondary after-effect of this motivation constitutes the present habit, which suffices to perpetuate the action in the same way as a body which has been set in motion by a thrust needs no further thrust to keep it in motion but will go on for all eternity provided it encounters no obstruction. The same applies to animals, in that their training is an enforced habit. The horse passively pulls its cart on and on without being driven: this motion is still the effect of the blow of the whip which first sent it off, perpetuated as habit according to the law of inertia. – All this is really more than a mere metaphor: the things are identical – they are the will at very different stages of its objectivization, which just because it conforms with the same law of motion assumes such differing shapes.

3

Viva muchos años! is a common greeting in Spanish, and the wish for long life is very customary all over the world. This is no doubt to be explained, not by a knowledge of what life is like, but of what man is like in his intrinsic nature – namely the will to live.

4

Every parting is a foretaste of death, and every reunion a foretaste of resurrection. That is why even people who were indifferent to one another rejoice so much when they meet again after twenty or thirty years.

5

The reason the sudden announcement of a great piece of good fortune can easily prove fatal is that happiness and unhappiness is no more than the ratio between what we demand and what we receive, so that we are not sensible of the goods we possess or are quite certain of possessing as such; because all enjoyment is really only *negative*, only has the effect of removing a pain, while pain or evil, on the other hand, is the actual positive element and is felt directly. With possession, or the certain prospect of it, our demands straightway increase and this increases our capacity for further possessions and wider prospects. If, on the contrary, constant misfortune has contracted our spirit and reduced our demands to a minimum, we lack the capacity to receive a sudden piece of good fortune; for since it meets with no existing demands which neutralize it, it produces an apparently positive effect and thus acts with its full force: so that it can burst the spirit asunder, i.e. prove fatal.

6

Hope is the confusion of the desire for a thing with its probability.

He who is without hope is also without fear: this is the meaning of the expression 'desperate'. For it is natural to man to believe true what he desires to be true, and to believe it because he desires it; if this salutary and soothing quality in his nature is obliterated by repeated ill-fortune, and he is even brought to the point of believing that what he does not desire to happen must happen and what he desires to happen can never happen simply because he desires it, then this is the condition called despair.

7

There is an unconscious appositeness in the use of the word *person* to designate the human individual, as is done in all European languages: for *persona* really means an actor's mask, and it is true that no one reveals himself as he is; we all wear a mask and play a role.

8

When he suffers an injustice the natural man burns with a thirst for *revenge*, and it has often been said that revenge is sweet. This fact is confirmed by the many sacrifices that have been made simply for the sake of revenge and without any idea of gaining recompense. I should like to attempt a psychological explanation of this.

No suffering laid upon us by nature or chance or fate is so painful as that inflicted by the will of another. This is so because we recognize nature and chance as the primal masters of the world and we can see that what nature and chance do to us they would have done to anyone else, so that when our sufferings originate from this source what we bewail is rather the common lot of man than our own individual lot. Suffering caused by the will of another, on the other hand, includes a quite peculiar and bitter addition to the pain or injury itself, namely the consciousness of someone else's superiority, whether in point of strength or of cunning, together with that of one's own impotence. Recompense, if recompense is possible, can cure the injury done: but that bitter addition, the feeling 'and that is what I have to put up with from you' which often hurts more than the injury itself, can be neutralized only by revenge. By returning the injury, either by force or by cunning, we demonstrate our superiority over him who has injured us and thereby annul the proof he gave of his superiority over us. Thus the heart acquires the satisfaction it thirsted for. Where, consequently, there is much pride or much vanity there will also be much revengefulness. But, as every fulfilled desire reveals itself more or less as a delusion, so does that for revenge. Usually the pleasure we hoped for from it is made bitter by the pity we afterwards feel; indeed, an exacted revenge will often subsequently break the heart and torment the conscience: we no longer feel the motivation which drove us to it, but the proof of our wickedness remains visibly before us.

9

Money is human happiness *in abstracto*; consequently he who is no longer capable of happiness *in concreto* sets his whole heart on money.

10

When will crowds out knowledge we call the result *obstinacy*.

11

Hatred is a thing of the heart, *contempt* a thing of the head.

Hatred and contempt are decidedly antagonistic towards one another and mutually exclusive. A great deal of hatred, indeed, has no other source than a compelled respect for the superior qualities of some other person; conversely, if you were to consider hating every miserable wretch you met you would have your work cut out: it is much easier to despise them one and all. True, genuine contempt, which is the obverse of true, genuine pride, stays hidden away in secret and lets no one suspect its existence: for if you let a person you despise notice the fact, you thereby reveal a certain respect for him, inasmuch as you want him to know how low you rate him – which betrays not contempt but hatred, which excludes contempt and only affects it. Genuine contempt, on the other hand, is the unsullied conviction of the worthlessness of another; it permits of indulgence and forbearance, in that for the sake of one's own peace and security one refrains from provoking the person despised, since everyone is capable of causing injury. If, however, this pure, cold and sincere contempt does ever reveal itself, it is requited with the most sanguinary hatred, because it is not within the power of the person despised to requite it with contempt.

12

What makes men *hard-hearted* is that everyone has sufficient troubles of his own to bear, or thinks he has. What, on the other hand, makes them so *inquisitive* is the polar opposite of suffering – boredom.

13

If you want to know how you really feel about someone take note of the impression an unexpected letter from him makes on you when you first see it on the doormat.

14

Reason deserves also to be called a *prophet*, for it holds the future up to us (namely as the coming consequence and effect of what we are now doing). This is precisely why it is calculated to keep us in check when lustful desires or outbursts of rage or avariciousness threaten to mislead us into courses which we would later be bound to regret.

15

States of human happiness and good fortune can as a rule be compared with certain groups of trees: seen from a distance they look beautiful, but if you go up to and into them their beauty disappears and you can no longer discover it. That is why we so often feel envy for other people.

16

Why, despite all our mirrors, do we never really know what we look like, and consequently cannot picture ourselves in imagination, as we can everyone else we know?

The reason is undoubtedly in part the fact that when we look at ourselves in a mirror we always do so with a direct and unmoving gaze, whereby the play of the eyes, which is so meaningful and in fact the actual characteristic of our gaze, is in great part lost. With this physical impossibility, however, there seems to go an analogous ethical impossibility. The condition under which *objective* comprehension of something perceived is possible is *alienation* from that which is perceived; but when we see our own reflection in a mirror we are unable to take an alienated view of it, because this view depends ultimately on moral egoism, with its profound feeling of *not me*: so that when we see our own reflection our egoism whispers to us a precautionary 'This is not not-me, but me', which has the effect of a *noli me tangere* and prevents any purely objective comprehension.

17

Unconscious existence possesses reality only for other beings in whose consciousness it appears: *immediate* reality is conditional upon individual consciousness. Thus the individual real existence of man also lies first and foremost in his *consciousness*. But this is as such necessarily ideational,[1] and thus conditioned by the intellect and by the sphere and substance of the intellect's activity. The degree of clarity of consciousness, and consequently of thought, can therefore be regarded as the degree of *reality of existence*. But this degree of thought, or of clear consciousness of one's own existence and of that of others, varies very greatly within the human race itself according to the measure of natural intellectual power, the extent to which this has been developed, and the amount of leisure available for reflection.

So far as intrinsic and inborn differences in intellectual power are concerned, these cannot very well be compared without considering each individual case, because such differences are not visible from a distance and not so easily discernible as distinctions in respect of culture, leisure and employment. But even going by these alone, it has to be admitted that many a man possesses at least a tenfold greater *degree of existence* than another – *exists* ten times as much.

There is no need to speak of savages whose life is often no more than one stage above that of the apes in the trees: consider for instance a porter in Naples or Venice (in the north the need to guard against the winter already makes men more thoughtful), and regard the course of his life from its beginning to its

1. *Ein Vorstellendes.*

end. Driven by want, sustained by his own strength, supplying the needs of the day, indeed of the hour, through his own labour; a great deal of exertion, constant turmoil, a great deal of hardship; no care for the morrow, refreshing rest after exhaustion, much wrangling and brawling, not a moment to spare for reflection, sensual ease in a mild climate and with tolerable food; finally, as the metaphysical element, some crass superstition provided by the Church. This restless, confused dream constitutes the life of millions of men. They *know* only for the purposes of their present *wants*: they give no thought to the coherence of their existence, not to speak of that of existence itself: to a certain extent they exist without really being aware of it.

Now consider the prudent, sensible merchant, who passes his life in speculations, cautiously carries out well-considered plans, establishes his house, makes provision for wife, child and heirs and also takes an active part in public affairs. This man obviously exists with very much more consciousness than the former: i.e. his existence possesses a higher degree of reality.

Next, observe the scholar, one for instance who explores the history of the past. This man will be conscious of the existence of the whole, beyond the era of his own existence, beyond his own person: he ponders the course of the world.

And finally the poet, and even more the philosopher, in whom thought has attained such a degree that, neglecting individual phenomena *in* existence, he stands in wonder before *existence itself*, before this mighty sphinx, and makes of it his problem. Consciousness has in him risen to such a degree of clarity that it has become universal consciousness, through which in him idea has stepped beyond all relation to the service of his will and now holds up to him a world which challenges him rather to investigation and contemplation than to involvement in its activities. – If, now, degrees of consciousness are degrees of reality – then when we call such a man the 'most real being' the phrase will have sense and meaning.

18

Why is 'common' an expression of contempt? 'uncommon, exceptional' one of approval? Why is everything common contemptible?

The original meaning of *common* is that which pertains to all, i.e. to the entire species. Consequently, he who possesses no further qualities than those pertaining to the human species in general is a *common man*.

For what value can be possessed by a being which is no different from millions of his kind? Millions? an infinity rather, an endless number of beings ceaselessly spurted forth by nature out of its inexhaustible well *in saecula saeculorum*,[2] as generous with them as the blacksmith is with sparks.

I have often argued that, while animals possess only a species character, man alone receives an actual individual character. Yet in most people there is only very little that is truly individual: they can be almost entirely divided into classes. Their desires and thoughts, like their faces, are those of the whole species, or at any rate of the class of man to which they belong, and are for that very reason trivial, everyday, common, thousandfold repeated. What they say and do can likewise usually be predicted in advance with a fair degree of accuracy. They have no individual quality: they are factory-made.

As their being is comprised in that of the species, should their existence not be so too? What goes without saying, however, is that every lofty, great, noble being will in consequence of his nature stand isolated in a world in which, to designate what is low and objectionable, no better expression could be found than that which means of ordinary occurrence: 'common'.

19

The will, as the thing in itself, is the common stuff of all beings, the universal element of things: consequently we possess it in common with each and every man, indeed with the animals,

2. To all eternity.

and even further on down. In the will as such we are consequently all similar, in so far as everything and everyone is filled and distended with will. On the other hand, that which exalts being above being, man above man, is knowledge. For that reason what we say should as far as possible be limited to expressions of knowledge. For the *will*, as that which is *common* to all, is for that reason also *common*: consequently, every vehement emergence of will is *common*, i.e. it demeans us to a mere exemplar of the species, for we then exhibit only the character of the species. What is common therefore is all anger, unbounded joy, all hatred, all fear, in short every emotion, i.e. every agitation of the will, if it becomes so strong as decisively to preponderate over knowledge in the consciousness and to allow a man to appear more as a willing than a knowing being. If he surrenders to such an emotion the greatest genius becomes equal to the commonest son of earth. He, on the other hand, who wants to be altogether uncommon, that is to say great, must never let a preponderant agitation of will take his consciousness over altogether, however much he is urged to do so. He must, e.g., be able to take note of the odious opinion of another without feeling his own aroused by it: indeed, there is no surer sign of greatness than ignoring hurtful or insulting expressions by attributing them without further ado, like countless other errors, to the speaker's lack of knowledge and thus merely taking note of them without feeling them.

20

Everything primary, and consequently everything genuine, in man works as the forces of nature do, *unconsciously*. What has passed through the consciousness thereby becomes an idea: consequently the expression of it is to a certain extent the communication of an idea. It follows that all the genuine and proved qualities of the character and the mind are primarily unconscious and only as such do they make a deep impression. What man performs unconsciously costs him no effort, and no effort can provide a substitute for it: it is in this fashion that all original conceptions such as lie at the bottom of every genuine achievement and constitute its kernel come into being. Thus only what is inborn is genuine and sound: if you want to achieve something in business, in writing, in painting, in anything, you must *follow the rules without knowing them.*

21

Many undoubtedly owe their good fortune to the circumstance that they possess a pleasing smile with which they win hearts. Yet these hearts would do better to beware and to learn from Hamlet's tables that one may smile, and smile, and be a villain.

22

People with great and splendid qualities make very little ado about admitting their faults and weaknesses. They regard them as something they have paid for, or they even go so far as to think that, far from being shamed by such weaknesses, they are doing these weaknesses honour by possessing them. This will especially be the case when these faults are those which go with their great qualities, as *conditiones sine quibus non.* As George Sand says: *chacun a les défauts de ses vertus.*

On the other hand, there are people of good character and irreproachable intelligence who never admit their few minor weaknesses, but carefully conceal them rather and are very sensitive to any allusion to them: the reason is that their whole merit lies in the absence of faults and defects, so that every fault that comes to light directly diminishes it.

23

If your abilities are only mediocre, *modesty* is mere honesty; but if you possess great talents, it is hypocrisy.

24

Man excels all the animals even in his *ability to be trained*. Moslems are trained to turn their faces towards Mecca five times a day and pray: they do so steadfastly. Christians are trained to cross themselves on certain occasions, to genuflect, etc.; while religion in general constitutes the real masterpiece in the art of training, namely the training of the mental capacities – which, as is well known, cannot be started too early. There is no absurdity so palpable that one could not fix it firmly in the head of every man on earth provided one began to imprint it before his sixth year by ceaselessly rehearsing it before him with solemn earnestness. For the training of men, as of animals, can be completely successful only in early youth.

25

To possess a great deal of *imagination* means that the *perceiving function of the brain* is sufficiently strong not invariably to require stimulation by the senses in order to become active.

The imagination is, consequently, the more active the fewer perceptions from without are transmitted to us by the senses. Protracted solitude, in prison or in a sick-bed, silence, twilight, darkness are conducive to it: under their influence it comes into play without being summoned. On the other hand, when a great deal of real material is provided from without for us to perceive, as on journeys, in the bustle of life, at high noon, then the imagination takes a holiday and refuses to become active even when summoned: it sees that this is not its season.

Nonetheless, if the imagination is to be fruitful it must have received a great deal of material from the outer world, for this alone can fill its store-room. But the nourishing of the fantasy is like the nourishing of the body: it is precisely at the time it is being given a great deal of nourishment which it has to digest that the body is at its least efficient and most likes to take a holiday – yet it is to this nourishment that it owes all the strength which later, in the right season, it manifests.

26

The *memory* may well become confused by what is put into it, but it cannot really become surfeited. Its capacity is not reduced by receiving, any more than arranging sand into different shapes reduces its capacity to receive other shapes. In this sense the memory is bottomless. Yet the more knowledge you possess, and the more multifarious it is, the more time you will require to find in your memory precisely what it is you want, because you will then be like a storekeeper who is trying to find one particular article in a large, variously stocked store; or, to speak correctly, because out of the very large number of trains of thought possible to you, you have to call up precisely *that* train which by virtue of previous exercise leads to the desired memory. For the memory is not a store-room for preserving things, it is only the capacity for exercising the mental powers: the head possesses knowledge only *potentia*, not *actu*.

27

People of very great ability will as a rule get on better with people of very limited ability than they will with people of ordinary ability, for the same reason as the despot and the plebeian, the grandparents and the grandchildren are natural allies.

28

People need external activity because they have no internal activity. Where, on the contrary, the latter does exist, the former is likely to be a very troublesome, indeed execrable annoyance and impediment. – The former fact also explains the restlessness of those who have nothing to do, and their aimless travelling. What drives them from country to country is the same boredom which at home drives them together into such crowds and heaps it is funny to see. I once received a choice confirmation of this truth from a gentleman of 50 with whom I was not acquainted, who told me about a two-year pleasure trip he had taken to distant lands and strange parts of the earth. When I remarked that he must have endured many difficulties, hardships and dangers, he replied very naïvely, without hesitation or preamble but as if merely enunciating the conclusion of a syllogism: 'I wasn't bored for an instant.'

ON RELIGION

I

Faith and Knowledge. Philosophy, as a science, has nothing whatever to do with what should or may be *believed*, it has to do only with what can be *known*. If this should turn out to be something quite other than what one is supposed to believe that is no disadvantage even for the belief, since it is the nature of belief to teach what cannot be known. If it could be known, belief would be ludicrous and useless: it would be, for instance, as if one should propound a theory to be held by faith in the field of mathematics.

It can, on the other hand, be objected that faith can teach more, much more, than philosophy; yet it can teach nothing which could be combined with the conclusion of philosophy, because knowledge is of a harder stuff than faith, so that when they collide the latter is shattered.

In any event, faith and knowledge are totally different things which for their mutual benefit have to be kept strictly separate, so that each goes its own way without paying the slightest attention to the other.

2

Revelation. The ephemeral generations of man are born and pass away in quick succession; individual men, burdened with fear, want and sorrow, dance into the arms of death. As they do so they never weary of asking what it is that ails them and what the whole tragi-comedy is supposed to mean. They call on Heaven for an answer, but Heaven stays silent. Instead of a voice from Heaven there come along priests with revelations.

But he is still in his childhood who can think that super-human beings have ever given our race information about the aim of its existence or that of the world. There are no other revelations than the thoughts of the wise, even if these – subject to error, as are all things human – are often clothed in strange allegories and myths and are then called religions. To this extent, therefore, it is all one whether you live and die trusting in your own thoughts or in those of others, for you are never trusting in anything but human thoughts and human opinion. Yet as a rule men have a weakness for putting their trust in those who pretend to supernatural sources of knowledge rather than in their own heads; but if you bear in mind the enormous intellectual inequality between man and man, then the thoughts of one may very well count with another as a revelation.

The fundamental, secret and primal piece of astuteness of all priests, everywhere and at all times, whether Brahmin or Mohammedan or Buddhist or Christian, is as follows. They have recognized and grasped the enormous strength and the ineradicability of the metaphysical need of man: they then pretend to possess the means of satisfying it, in that the solution to the great enigma has, by extraordinary channels, been directly communicated to them. Once they have persuaded men of the truth of this, they can lead and dominate them to their heart's content. The more prudent rulers enter into an alliance with them: the others are themselves ruled by them. If, however, as the rarest of all exceptions, a philosopher comes to the throne, the whole comedy is disrupted in the most unseemly fashion.

3

On Christianity. To arrive at a just judgement of Christianity one must consider what preceded it and what it supplanted. First and foremost Graeco-Roman paganism: considered as popular metaphysics a very trivial affair, without any real, distinct dogmas, without any categorical ethic, indeed without any real moral tendency, and without sacred scriptures: so that it hardly deserves to be called a religion at all – it is rather a play of fantasy, a production cobbled together by poets out of popular legends, and for the most part an obvious personification of natural forces. It is hard to imagine that grown men ever took this childish religion seriously: yet there are many passages in ancient writers which suggest that they did, notably the first book of Valerius Maximus [1] but even a good many passages in Herodotus. In later times and with the advance of philosophy such serious credence vanished, which made it possible for Christianity to supplant this state religion in spite of its external supports. – The second thing Christianity had to supplant was Judaism, whose rude dogma was sublimated and tacitly allegorized in the Christian. Christianity is in general definitely of an allegorical nature: for what in profane matters is called allegory is in religions called mystery. It has to be conceded that Christianity is much superior to both these earlier religions not only as regards *morality*, in which it alone (so far as the Occident is concerned) teaches *caritas*, reconciliation, love of one's enemy, resignation and denial of one's own will, but even as regards *dogma*: it is best, however, to communicate this to the great masses, who are incapable of grasping truth directly, in the form of a beautiful allegory, which completely suffices them as a guide to practical living and as an anchor of consolation and hope. But a small addition of absurdity is a necessary ingredient in such an allegory: it serves to indicate its allegorical nature. If you take Christian dogma *sensu proprio*, then Voltaire is right. Taken allegorically, on the other hand, it is a sacred myth, a vehicle for bringing to the people truths which would otherwise be altogether inaccessible to them. Even the Church's assertion that reason is totally incompetent and blind with respect to the dogmas of religion and must be repudiated means at bottom that these dogmas are of an allegorical nature and therefore not to be judged by the standards which reason, which takes everything *sensu proprio*, can alone apply. The absurdities of dogma are precisely the mark and sign of the allegorical and mythical, even though in the present case they arise from the need to link together two such heterogeneous doctrines as those of the Old and the New Testaments. This great allegory first came about gradually through the interpretation of external and chance circum-

1. *Fl.* about A.D. 20: his book, *Factorum et dictorum memorabilium* (about A.D. 31), remained popular almost until modern times.

stances under the silent influence of a deep-lying truth not clearly present in the consciousness, until it was finally completed by Augustine, who penetrated most deeply into its meaning and was then able to comprehend it as a systematic whole and to supply what was lacking in it. Thus the complete and perfect Christian doctrine is that of Augustine, as also affirmed by Luther, and not, as present-day Protestants who, taking 'revelation' *sensu proprio* confine it to *one* individual, think, primitive Christianity – (just as it is not the seed but the fruit which is edible). – Yet the weak point of all religions remains that they can never dare to confess to being allegorical, so that they have to present their doctrines in all seriousness as true *sensu proprio*; which, because of the absurdities essential to allegory, leads to perpetual deception and a great disadvantage for religion. What is even worse, indeed, is that in time it comes to light that they are *not* true *sensu proprio*, and then they perish. To this extent it would be better to admit their allegorical nature straightway: only the difficulty here is to make the people understand that a thing can be true and not true at the same time. But since we find that all religions are constituted to a greater or less degree in this way, we have to recognize that the absurd is to a certain extent appropriate to the human race, indeed an element of its life, and that deception is indispensable to it – a fact which is confirmed in other directions.

Evidence for and an example of the above-mentioned origin of absurdities in the union of the Old Testament and the New is provided by, among other things, the Christian doctrine of predestination and grace perfected by Luther's guiding star, Augustine: according to this doctrine one man has the advantage over another of being the object of divine grace, which amounts to coming into the world possessed of a ready-made privilege, and one in respect of the most important matter of all. The offensiveness and absurdity of this doctrine originates, however, entirely in the presupposition, derived from the Old Testament, that man is the work of an external will, which called him up out of nothing. But considering that genuine moral superiority actually is inborn, the matter appears in a quite different and more rational light under the Brahmanic and Buddhist presupposition of metempsychosis, according to which whatever advantages a man may be born with he has brought with him from another world and an earlier life, so that they are not a gift of grace but the fruit of his own deeds performed in that other world. – To this dogma of Augustine there is, however, joined this worse one, that out of the mass of mankind, who are corrupt and thus doomed to everlasting damnation, a very small number are, as a consequence of predestination and election by grace, acquitted and will consequently be saved, while deserved destruction and the eternal torments of Hell will be visited on the rest. Taken *sensu proprio* the dogma here becomes revolting, for not only does it punish the faults, or even the mere lack of faith, of a life often hardly more than twenty years long with torments which have no end, it also adds that this almost universal damnation is actually the effect of original sin, and thus the necessary consequence of man's first Fall. But this must have been foreseen by at any rate him who firstly failed to make men better than they are and then set a trap for them into which he must have known they would fall, since everything was his work and nothing was hidden from him. According to this dogma, then, he called into existence out of nothing a weak and sin-prone race in order to hand it over to endless torment. There is finally the further fact that the God who prescribes forbearance and forgiveness of every sin, even to the point of loving one's enemy, fails to practise it himself, but does rather the opposite: since a punishment which is introduced at the end of things, when all is over and done with for ever, can be intended neither to improve nor deter; it is nothing but revenge. Thus regarded, it seems that the entire race is in fact definitely intended and expressly created for eternal torment and damnation – all, that is, apart from those few exceptions which are rescued from this fate by divine grace, although one knows not why. These aside, it appears as if the dear Lord created the world for the benefit of the Devil – in which event he would have done far better not to have created it at all. – This is what happens to dogmas when you take them *sensu proprio*: understood *sensu allegorico*, on the other hand, all this is susceptible of a more satisfactory interpretation. What is absurd, indeed revolting, in this doctrine is however, as has already been said, first and foremost merely a consequence of Judaic theism, with its creation from nothing and that which goes with it, the really paradoxical and scandalous denial of the natural doctrine of metempsychosis, a doctrine which is to a certain extent self-evident and which has therefore been in all ages accepted by virtually the entire human race with the exception of the Jews. It was precisely to obviate the colossal disadvantage arising from this rejection of metempsychosis and to moderate the revolting nature of the dogma that in the sixth century Pope Gregory I very wisely developed the doctrine of Purgatory (which is, in its essentials, to be found as early as Origen[2]) and formally incorporated it into the teaching of the Church; whereby a kind of substitute for metempsychosis was introduced into Christianity, inasmuch as both constitute a process of purification. It was with the same objective in view that the doctrine of the restoration of all things was instituted, according to which even the sinners are one and all restituted *in integrum* in the last act of the universal comedy. Only the Protestants, with their obstinate Bible religion, have refused to let themselves be deprived of everlasting punishment in Hell. Much good may it do 'em – one might say maliciously: the consolation is, however, that they do not really believe in it; for the moment they are leaving that subject alone, thinking in their hearts: Oh, it won't be as bad as all that.

The Augustinian conception of the enormous number of the sinners and the very small number of those who deserve eternal bliss, which is in itself a correct conception, is also to be discovered in Brahmanism and Buddhism, where, however, the doctrine of metempsychosis robs it of its repellent character. It is true that in the former final redemption and in the latter Nirvana is also granted to very few, but these do not come into the world specially chosen and privileged, their deserts are those they have acquired in a previous life and which they continue to

2. Origenes Adamantius (*c*. 185–*c*. 254), theologian.

maintain in the present one. The rest, however, are not cast into the everlasting pit of Hell, they are transported to the kind of world which is in keeping with their deeds. If, consequently, you should ask the propounders of these religions where and what all those who have not attained to redemption are, they would reply: 'Look around you: here is where they are, this is what they are: this is their arena, this is Sansara, i.e. the world of desire, of birth, of pain, of age, of sickness and of death.' – On the other hand, if this Augustinian dogma of the tiny number of the elect and the great number of the eternally damned is understood merely *sensu allegorico* and interpreted in the sense of our own philosophy, then it agrees with the fact that only very few achieve denial of the will and thereby redemption from this world (as in Buddhism only very few achieve Nirvana). What, on the other hand, this dogma hypostatizes as eternal damnation is nothing other than this world of ours: *this* is what devolves upon all the rest. It is a sufficiently evil place: it is Purgatory, it is Hell, and devils are not lacking in it. Only consider what men sometimes inflict upon men, with what ingenious torments one will slowly torture another to death, and ask yourself whether devils could do more. And sojourn in this place is likewise eternal for all those who obdurately persist in affirming the will to live.

But in truth, if one from Asia should ask me what Europe is, I would have to reply: it is the continent utterly possessed by the unheard-of and incredible delusion that the birth of man is his absolute beginning and that he is created out of nothing.

Fundamentally, and both their mythologies apart, Buddha's *Sansara* and *Nirvana* are identical with Augustine's two *civitates* into which the world is divided, the *civitas terrena* and *coelestis*.[3]

The *Devil* is in Christianity a very necessary personage, as counterweight to the all-goodness, omniscience and omnipotence of God: it is impossible to see where the predominating, incalculable and boundless evil of the world is supposed to come from if the Devil is not there to assume responsibility for it. Since the

3. The City of this world and the City of God.

Rationalists have abolished him, the disadvantage to the other side accruing from his absence has grown greater and greater and more and more evident: which could have been foreseen and was foreseen by the orthodox. For you cannot remove one pillar from a building without endangering the rest. – This also confirms what has been established elsewhere, that Jehovah is a transformation of Ormuzd and Satan of Ahriman, who is inseparable from him: Ormuzd himself, however, is a transformation of Indra.

Christianity possesses the peculiar disadvantage that, unlike the other religions, it is not a pure *doctrine*, but essentially and above all a *history*, a succession of events, a complex of facts and the actions and sufferings of individuals, and it is this history which constitutes the dogma belief in which redeems.

Another fundamental error of Christianity is that it has in an unnatural fashion sundered mankind from the *animal world* to which it essentially belongs and now considers mankind alone as of any account, regarding the animals as no more than *things*. This error is a consequence of creation out of nothing, after which the Creator, in the first and second chapters of Genesis, takes all the animals just as if they were things, and without so much as the recommendation to kind treatment which even a dog-seller usually adds when he parts with his dogs, hands them over to man for man to *rule*, that is to do with them what he likes; subsequently, in the second chapter, the Creator goes on to appoint him the first professor of zoology by commissioning him to give the animals the names they shall thenceforth bear, which is once more only a symbol of their total dependence on him, i.e. their total lack of rights.

It can truly be said: Men are the devils of the earth, and the animals are the tormented souls. This is the consequence of that installation scene in the Garden of Eden. For the mob can be controlled only by force or by religion, and here Christianity leaves us shamefully in the lurch. I heard from a reliable source that a Protestant pastor, requested by an animal protection society to preach a sermon against cruelty to animals, replied that with the best will in the world he was unable to do so, because he could find no support in his religion. The man was honest, and he was right.

When I was studying at Göttingen, Blumenbach spoke to us very seriously about the horrors of vivisection and told us what a cruel and terrible thing it was; wherefore it should be resorted to only very seldom and for very important experiments which would bring immediate benefit, and even then it must be carried out as publicly as possible so that the cruel sacrifice on the altar of science should be of the maximum possible usefulness. Nowadays, on the contrary, every little medicine-man thinks he has the right to torment animals in the cruellest fashion in his torture chamber so as to decide problems whose answers have for long stood written in books into which he is too lazy and ignorant to stick his nose. – Special mention should be made of an abomination committed by Baron Ernst von Bibra at Nürnberg and, with incomprehensible *naïveté, tanquam re bene gesta*,[4] narrated by him to the public in his *Vergleichende Untersuchungen über das Gehirn des Menschen und der Wirbelthiere*[5]: he deliberately let two rabbits *starve to death*! – in order to undertake the totally idle and useless experiment of seeing whether starvation produces a proportional change in the chemical composition of the brain! For the ends of science – *n'est-ce pas*? Have these gentlemen of the scalpel and crucible no notion at all then that they are first and foremost men, and chemists only secondly? How can you sleep soundly knowing you have harmless animals under lock and key in order to starve them slowly to death? Don't you wake up screaming in the night?

It is obviously high time that the Jewish conception of nature, at any rate in regard to animals, should come to an end in

4. As if the thing were done well.
5. *Comparative Experiments on the Brain of Man and Vertebrate Animals* (Mannheim, 1854).

Europe, and that *the eternal being which, as it lives in us, also lives in every animal* should be recognized as such, and as such treated with care and consideration. One must be blind, deaf and dumb, or completely chloroformed by the *foetor judaicus*, not to see that the animal is in essence absolutely the same thing that we are, and that the difference lies merely in the accident, the intellect, and not in the substance, which is the will.

The greatest benefit conferred by the railways is that they spare millions of draught-horses their miserable existence.

4

On Theism. Just as polytheism is the personification of individual departments and forces of nature, so monotheism is the personification of the whole of nature at one blow.

But when I try to imagine myself standing before an individual being and saying to him: 'My creator! Once I was nothing: but you have brought me forth, so that now I am something, and what that something is is myself' – and then adding: 'Thank you for this favour' – and even concluding with: 'If I have been good for nothing, that is *my* fault' – then I must confess that, as a consequence of my philosophical and Indian studies, my head has become incapable of sustaining such a thought. And this thought is moreover a counterpart of that which Kant presents us in the *Critique of Pure Reason* (in the section on the impossibility of a cosmological proof): 'One cannot resist the thought, although neither can one endure it, that a being which we imagine as the highest of all possible beings says as it were to himself: I am from eternity to eternity, there is nothing beside me except what exists purely through my will: *but whence am I then?*'

It is all one whether you make an idol of wood, stone, metal, or put it together out of abstract concepts: as soon as you have before you a personal being to whom you sacrifice, on whom you call, whom you thank, it is *idolatry*. It also makes little difference at bottom whether you sacrifice your sheep or your inclinations. Every rite, every prayer is an incontrovertible witness to *idolatry*. That is why mystical sects of all religions agree in doing away with all rites.

5

Old and New Testament. The basic character of Judaism is *realism* and *optimism*, which are closely related and the preconditions of actual *theism*, since they consider the material world absolutely real and life as a pleasing gift made expressly for us. The basic character of Brahmanism and Buddhism, on the contrary, is *idealism* and *pessimism*, since they allow the world only a dream-like existence and regard life as the consequence of our sins. In the doctrine of the Zend-Avesta,[6] from which Judaism is known to have derived, the pessimistic element is still present and represented by Ahriman. In Judaism, however, he is accorded only a subordinate position as Satan, who is nonetheless still, like Ahriman, the author of snakes, scorpions and vermin. Judaism employs him straightway to repair its fundamental error of optimism, namely to produce the Fall, which then introduces into that religion the pessimistic element required for the sake of fidelity to the most obvious of truths. This element is the most correct basic idea in the religion, although it transfers to the course of existence what ought to be represented as its ground and as preceding it.

The New Testament must be of Indian origin: witness of that is its altogether Indian ethic, in which morality leads to asceticism, its pessimism and its avatar. But it is for precisely this reason that it stands in decided intrinsic opposition to the Old Testament, so that the only thing in the Old Testament which could provide a connecting link with it was the story of the Fall. For when this Indian doctrine entered into the Promised Land there arose the task of uniting the knowledge of the corruption and misery of the world, of its need for redemption and of salvation through an avatar, together with the

6. Zoroastrianism.

morality of self-denial and atonement, with Jewish monotheism and its 'Behold, it was very good'. And this union was achieved, as far as it could be; as far, that is, as two so completely heterogeneous, indeed antithetical doctrines *can* be united.

The Creator from nothing, separate from the world, is identified with the Saviour and through him with mankind, whose representative he is, since mankind is redeemed in him as it once fell in Adam and has since lain enmeshed in sin, corruption, suffering and death. For this is how the world appears here as much as it does in Buddhism – and no longer in the light of the Jewish optimism which had found everything 'very good': the Devil himself is now styled 'Prince of this world' (John xii 31). The world is no longer an end, but a means: the kingdom of joy lies beyond it and beyond death. Renunciation in this world and the direction of all hope towards a better world constitutes the spirit of Christianity. The way to such a better world is, however, opened by reconciliation, i.e. redemption from the world and its ways. In morality, the *lex talionis* is replaced by the command to love one's enemy, the promise of a numberless posterity by the promise of eternal life, and the punishment of transgressions to the fourth generation by the Holy Ghost, beneath whose wings everything reposes.

Thus we see the doctrine of the Old Testament rectified and given a new meaning by that of the New, whereby it is made intrinsically and essentially to accord with the ancient religions of India. Everything true in Christianity is also to be discovered in Brahmanism and Buddhism. But the Jewish notion of an animated nothingness, a temporal product which can never be too humbly thankful for an ephemeral existence full of misery, fear and want, nor praise Jehovah too highly for it – this you will look for in vain in Hinduism and Buddhism.

If one wanted to venture on conjectures as to how this agreement with Indian doctrines came about, one might suggest that the Flight into Egypt may rest on some historical fact, and that Jesus was brought up by Egyptian priests, whose religion was of Indian origin, received Indian ethics and the concept of the avatar from them, and afterwards sought to adapt these doctrines to Jewish dogmas and to graft them on to the ancient tree. The feeling of his own moral and intellectual superiority may then have induced him to regard himself as an avatar and consequently to call himself the Son of Man so as to indicate that he was more than simply a man. It is even possible to think that, with the strength and purity of his will and by virtue of the omnipotence which pertains to will in general as thing in itself which we know from the fact of animal magnetism and other magical effects related to it, he was also able to perform so-called miracles, i.e. operate through the metaphysical influence of the will; in connexion with which the instruction he received from the Egyptian priests would likewise have stood him in good stead. Legend would subsequently have exaggerated the number and miraculousness of these miracles. It is only suppositions of this kind which can to some extent explain how Paul, whose principal epistles at least must be genuine, can seriously represent as God incarnate and as one with the Creator of the world a man who has died so recently that many of his contemporaries are still alive: for seriously meant apotheoses of this sort and magnitude usually require many centuries to come gradually to fruition. On the other hand, this consideration could serve as an argument against the genuineness of the Pauline epistles in general.

That the Gospels we possess rest upon an original or at any rate a fragment from the time of Jesus and from his circle I conclude from the objectionable prophecy of the end of the world and of the Lord's glorious Second Coming in the clouds, which is supposed to be going to take place during the lifetime of some of those present when it is promised. For that this promise remained unfulfilled is an extremely vexatious circumstance which proved a stumbling-block not only in later ages but caused embarrassment already to Peter and Paul. If the Gospels, a hundred or so years later, had been indited without the aid of contemporary documents, one would surely have guarded against introducing prophecies of this kind, the non-fulfilment of which had already been brought to light.

The principle laid down by Strauss[7] that the Gospel story, or at any rate its individual detail, is to be explained mythologically is certainly correct, and it will be hard to determine how far this principle extends. As to the nature of myths in general, it will be best to employ less delicate examples closer to hand. Thus, e.g., King Arthur was throughout the Middle Ages, in France as well as in England, a quite authentic person, known for many deeds and always appearing with the same character and the same entourage: with his Round Table, his knights, his heroic acts, his magician, his faithless wife and her Lancelot du Lac, etc., he constituted the standing theme of poets and romancers of many centuries, who all present us with the same characters and agree fairly well in the events they describe, and noticeably differ from one another only in costumes and customs, that is to say according to which age they belong to. Now a few years ago the French government sent M. de la Villemarqué to England to investigate the origin of these myths of King Arthur. The facts behind the myths turned out to be that a petty chieftain named Arthur lived in Wales at the beginning of the sixth century: he fought indefatigably against the invading Saxons, but his insignificant deeds have been forgotten. It is he, then, who, Heaven knows why, became the splendid personage celebrated for many centuries in countless songs, romances and stories.[8] The case is almost the same with Roland, who is the hero of the whole Middle Ages, celebrated in countless songs, epic poems and romances, and even statues,[9] until he was at last transfigured by Ariosto.[10] History, however, refers to him only once, and that only incidentally and in four

7. David Strauss (1808–74), theologian.

8. De la Villemarqué's conclusions were published in *Contes populaires des anciens Bretons, avec un essay sur l'origine des épopées sur la table ronde* (1842).

9. The stone statues of an armed warrior set up at Bremen and other cities to symbolize the Imperial power were called 'Roland in the marketplace' or 'Roland statues', and it may be these to which Schopenhauer is referring.

10. Ludovico Ariosto (1474–1533), poet: *Orlando furioso*, his masterpiece, is one of the greatest poems of the Renaissance (Orlando=Roland).

words: Eginhard includes him in the list of those who stayed behind at Roncesvalles as *Hroudlandus, Britannici limitis praefectus* – and that is all we know about him; just as all we really know about Jesus Christ is the passage in Tacitus.[11]

6

Sects. Augustinianism, with its dogma of original sin and what is associated with it, is, as has already been said, actual Christianity. Pelagianism, on the other hand, is the attempt to take Christianity back to crude and shallow Judaism and its optimism.

The antithesis between Augustinianism and Pelagianism has continually divided the Church: going down to their ultimate ground, one could say that the former speaks of the essence in itself of things, the latter of phenomena which it takes for essence. The Pelagian, e.g., denies original sin, since the child which has as yet done nothing whatever must be innocent: he does this because he does not see that, while the child is a beginning as phenomenon, it is not a beginning as thing in itself. The same consideration applies to free will, to the Saviour's propitiatory death, to grace, in short to everything. – In consequence of its comprehensibility and shallowness, Pelagianism always predominates, but it does so more than ever now, as Rationalism. The Greek Orthodox Church preaches a qualified Pelagianism, as, since the Council of Trent, does the Catholic Church, its object being to set itself in opposition to the Augustinian and consequently mystically minded Luther, and to Calvin: the Jesuits are no less semi-Pelagian. On the other hand, the Jansenists are Augustinian and their doctrine may well be the most genuine form of Christianity. For, by rejecting celibacy and asceticism in general, together with the saints, who are the representatives of asceticism, Protestantism has become a truncated, or rather decapitated Christianity whose apex is missing.

11. The name Christian 'was derived from Christ, who in the reign of Tiberius suffered under Pontius Pilate, the procurator of Judaea' (Tacitus: *Annals* XV, 44).

7

Rationalism. The fundamental distinction between religions does not lie in whether they are monotheistic, polytheistic, pantheistic or atheistic (as Buddhism is), but in whether they are optimistic or pessimistic. The Old and the New Testaments are for this reason diametrically opposed, and their union forms a very strange centaur: for the Old Testament is optimistic, the New Testament pessimistic. The former is a tune in the major, the latter a tune in the minor.

This basic character of Christianity, which Augustine, Luther and Melanchthon [12] perceived very truly and as far as possible systematized, our present-day Rationalists seek to expunge and exegesize away, so as to lead Christianity back to a prosaic, egoistic, optimistic Judaism, adding to it an improved morality and the future life demanded by a consistent optimism, so that the glorious time we are having shall not come to so early an end, and death, which cries out all too loudly against the optimistic outlook and comes at last like the stone guest to the feasting Don Juan, shall be done away with. – These Rationalists are honest but shallow people with no presentiment of the profound meaning of the New Testament myth, who cannot get beyond the optimism of Judaism. They want the plain, unvarnished truth in the domain of history as in that of dogma. They can be compared with the Euhemerists [13] of antiquity. What the supranaturalists bring us is, to be sure, fundamentally a mythology: but this mythology is the vehicle of important profound truths which cannot be conveyed to the understanding of the great masses in any other way. The common error of both parties is that they seek in religion the plain, unvarnished, literal truth. But the plain, unvarnished, literal truth is striven for only in philosophy: religion possesses only a truth suitable to

12. Philipp Melanchthon (1497–1560), theologian and religious reformer. His name is a Latinization of Schwarzerd (black earth).

13. Euhemerist derives from Euhemerus (*fl.* about 300 B.C.), who declared that the gods were deifications of human heroes and conquerors, i.e. that they were myths.

the people, an indirect, a symbolic, allegorical truth. Christianity is an allegory reflecting a true idea; but the allegory itself is not what is true. To take the allegory for the truth is the error which supranaturalists and Rationalists agree in making. The former will assert that the allegory is in itself true; the latter will twist and bend its meaning until they have, according to their own lights, made it true in itself. Each party is accordingly able to make pertinent and valid points against the other. The Rationalists say to the supranaturalists: 'Your doctrine isn't true.' The latter retort: 'Your doctrine isn't Christianity.' Both are right. The Rationalists believe they are taking reason as their standard: in fact, however, their standard is only reason caught up in the presuppositions of theism and optimism, rather like Rousseau's *Profession de foi du vicaire savoyard*, that prototype of all Rationalism. Of Christian dogma they will grant validity to nothing but what they hold true *sensu proprio*: namely, theism and the immortality of the soul. While supranaturalism possesses at any rate allegorical truth, Rationalism cannot be accorded any truth at all. The Rationalists are simply wrong. If you would be a Rationalist you will have to be a philosopher and as such emancipate yourself from all authority, stride forward and shrink at nothing. If, however, you would be a theologian you ought to be consistent and cleave to authority, even if it insists on your believing what is incomprehensible. A man cannot serve two masters: so it is either reason or the scriptures. The *juste milieu* here means falling between two stools. Either believe or philosophize! – whichever you choose, choose wholeheartedly. But to believe up to a certain point and no farther, and to philosophize up to a certain point and no farther – this is the halfheartedness which constitutes the fundamental trait of Rationalism.

Those who think the sciences can go on advancing and spreading wider and wider without threatening the continued existence and prosperity of religion are very much in error. Physics and metaphysics are the natural enemies of religion. To speak of peace and accord between them is very ludicrous:

it is a *bellum ad internecionem*.[14] Religions are the children of ignorance, and they do not long survive their mother. Omar understood that when he burned the library at Alexandria: his reason for doing so – that the knowledge contained in the books was either also contained in the Koran or was superfluous – is regarded as absurd, but is in fact very shrewd if taken *cum grano salis*: it signifies that if the sciences go beyond the Koran they are enemies of religion and consequently not to be tolerated. Christianity would be in much better shape today if Christian rulers had been as wise as Omar. By now, however, it is a little late to burn all the books.

Mankind is growing out of religion as out of its childhood clothes. Faith and knowledge do not get on well together in the same head: they are like a wolf and a sheep in the same cage – and knowledge is the wolf which threatens to eat up its companion. – In its death throes, we see religion clinging to morality, whose mother it would like to pretend to be. In vain! – genuine morality is dependent on no religion, although religion sanctions and thereby sustains it.

Belief is like love: it cannot be compelled; and as any attempt to compel love produces hate, so it is the attempt to compel belief which first produces real unbelief.

8

The reason civilization is at its highest point among *Christian* peoples is not that Christianity is favourable to it but that Christianity is dead and no longer exercises much influence: as long as it did exercise influence, civilization was at a very low point among Christian peoples. All *religion* is antagonistic towards culture.

What a bad conscience religion must have is to be judged by the fact that it is forbidden under pain of such severe punishment to *mock* it.

14. War of extermination.

1

WRITERS can be divided into meteors, planets and fixed stars. The first produce a momentary effect: you gaze up, cry: 'Look!' – and then they vanish for ever. The second, the moving stars, endure for much longer. By virtue of their proximity they often shine more brightly than the fixed stars, which the ignorant mistake them for. But they too must soon vacate their place, they shine moreover only with a borrowed light, and their sphere of influence is limited to their own fellow travellers (their contemporaries). The third alone are unchanging, stand firm in the firmament, shine by their own light and influence all ages equally, in that their aspect does not alter when our point of view alters since they have no parallax. Unlike the others, they do not belong to one system (nation) alone: they belong to the Universe. But it is precisely because they are so high that their light usually takes so many years to reach the eyes of dwellers on earth.

2

There are above all two kinds of writer: those who write for the sake of what they have to say and those who write for the sake of writing. The former have had ideas or experiences which seem to them worth communicating; the latter need money and that is why they write – for money. They think for the purpose of writing. You can recognize them by the fact that they spin out their ideas to the greatest possible extent, that their ideas are half-true, obscure, forced and vacillating, and that they usually prefer the twilight so as to appear what they are not, which is why their writings lack definiteness and clarity. You can soon see they are writing simply in order to cover paper:

and as soon as you do see it you should throw the book down, for time is precious. – Payment and reserved copyright are at bottom the ruin of literature. Only he who writes entirely for the sake of what he has to say writes anything worth writing. It is as if there were a curse on money: every writer writes badly as soon as he starts writing for gain. The greatest works of the greatest men all belong to a time when they had to write them for nothing or for very small payment: so that here too the Spanish proverb holds good: *Honra y provecho no caben en un saco*.[1]

A multitude of bad writers lives exclusively on the stupid desire of the public to read nothing but what has just been printed: the journalists. Well named! In English the word means 'day-labourers'.

3

And then again, there can be said to be three kinds of author. Firstly, there are those who write without thinking. They write from memory, from reminiscence, or even directly from other people's books. This class is the most numerous. – Secondly, there are those who think while writing. They think in order to write. Very common. – Thirdly, there are those who have thought before they started writing. They write simply because they have thought. Rare.

Even among the small number of writers who actually think seriously before they start writing, there are extremely few who think about *the subject itself*: the rest merely think about *books*, about what others have said about the subject. They require, that is to say, the close and powerful stimulation of ideas produced by other people in order to think at all. These ideas are then their immediate theme, so that they remain constantly under their influence and consequently never attain to true originality. The above-mentioned minority, on the other hand, are stimulated to think by the subject itself, so that their think-

1. Honour and money don't belong in the same purse.

ing is directed immediately to this. Among them alone are to be discovered those writers who endure and become immortal.

Only he who takes what he writes directly out of his own head is worth reading.

4

A book can never be more than a reproduction of the thoughts of its author. The value of these thoughts lies either in the *material*, that is in what he has thought *upon*, or in the *form*, i.e. the way in which the material is treated, that is in *what* he has thought upon it.

The *upon what* is manifold, as are the advantages it bestows on books. All empirical material, that is everything historically or physically factual in itself and in the widest sense, belongs here. The characteristic quality lies in the *object*, so that the book can be an important one whoever its author may be.

In the case of the *what*, on the other hand, the characteristic quality lies in the *subject*. The topics treated can be such as are accessible and familiar to all men, but it is the form in which they are comprehended, the *what* of the thought, which here bestows value, and this lies in the subject. If, consequently, a book of this sort is admirable and unique, its author is so too; from which it follows that the merit of a writer who is worth reading is the greater the less it owes to his material, and even the more familiar and much-employed this material is. Thus, e.g., the three great Greek tragedians all employed the same material.

Thus when a book becomes famous you should firmly distinguish whether it is on account of its material or on account of its form.

The public is much more interested in the material than in the form. It displays this tendency in its most ridiculous shape in regard to poetic works, in that it painstakingly tracks down the real events or personal circumstances which occasioned the work, and these, indeed, become more interesting to it than the works themselves, so that it reads more *about* than *by* Goethe and studies the Faust legend more assiduously than *Faust*. And if Bürger once said: 'They will undertake learned research into who Lenore really was',[2] we have seen this literally come to pass in the case of Goethe. – This preference for the material as against the form is as if one should ignore the form and painting of a beautiful Etruscan vase in order to carry out a chemical analysis of the pigment and clay.

5

The actual life of a thought lasts only until it reaches the point of speech: there it petrifies and is henceforth dead but indestructible, like the petrified plants and animals of prehistory. As soon as our thinking has found words it ceases to be sincere or at bottom serious. When it begins to exist for others it ceases to live in us, just as the child severs itself from its mother when it enters into its own existence.

6

Literary periodicals ought to be the dam against the ever-rising flood of bad and unprofitable books produced by the unprincipled scribbling of our age. With the incorruptibility, judiciousness and severity of their judgements, they should scourge without mercy all patchwork put together by incompetents, all the page-filling through which empty heads seek to fill their empty pockets, which is to say nine-tenths of all books, and thus work against triviality and imposture as their duty dictates; instead of which, they promote these things: and their abject tolerance allies itself with author and publisher to rob the public of its time and its money. Their writers are as a rule professors or *literati* who, because of low salaries or poor payment, write from need of money: so, since they all have a common aim, their interests are in common, they keep together, mutually sustain one another and speak in favour of one another: this is the

2. Gottfried August Bürger (1747–94), poet. His ballad *Lenore* (1773) is one of the most famous of all German poems.

origin of all the laudatory reviews of bad books which constitute the content of literary periodicals. Their motto ought to be: Live and let live!

Anonymity, that shield for every kind of literary scoundrelism, must disappear. The pretext for its introduction into literary periodicals was that it protected honest critics from the wrath of authors and their patrons. But for every case of this kind there are a hundred cases where it serves merely to allow complete irresponsibility to reviewers who would be unable to defend what they write, or even to conceal the shame of those so venal and abject as to recommend books to the public in exchange for a tip from their publisher. It often merely serves to cloak the obscurity, incompetence and insignificance of the reviewer. It is unbelievable what impudence these fellows are capable of, and from what degree of literary knavery they will not shrink, once they know themselves secure in the shadow of anonymity.

Rousseau already said in the preface to *La Nouvelle Héloïse*: '*Tout honnête homme doit avouer les livres qu'il publie*' – which means in English: 'Every honest man puts his name to what he writes', and universally affirmative propositions can be reversed *per contrapositionem*. How much more this applies to polemical writings, which reviews usually are!

7

Style is the physiognomy of the mind. It is less deceptive than that of the body. To imitate the style of another is to wear a mask, and however beautiful this may be its lifelessness soon makes it seem insipid and unendurable, so that the ugliest living face is preferable.

Stylistic affectation can be compared to pulling faces.

8

To arrive at a provisional assessment of a writer's worth it is not necessary to know *what* or *upon what* he has thought, because that would mean having to read everything he has written; it is sufficient in the first instance to know *how* he has thought. Now an exact impression of this *how* of his thinking, of its essential nature and prevailing *quality*, is provided by his style. For this reveals the *formal* nature of all a man's thoughts, which must always remain the same no matter *what* or *upon what* he thinks. It is, as it were, the paste from which he moulds all his figures, however various they may be. Just as Eulenspiegel, when asked how long it would take to reach the next town, gave his questioner the apparently senseless answer: 'Walk!' with a view to judging from his pace how far he would get in a certain time, so I read a couple of pages of an author and already know more or less how far I can profit from him.

The first rule, indeed by itself virtually a sufficient condition for good style, is *to have something to say*.

The dullness and tediousness of the writings of commonplace people might be a consequence of the fact that they are speaking only half-consciously, that is to say not really understanding the meaning of the words they use, since these are something they have learned and received finished and complete, so that what they put together is rather whole phrases (*phrases banales*) than individual words. This is the origin of the palpable lack of distinct ideas which characterize their writings, since they are without that which imposes distinctness on ideas, individual clear thinking: instead of this, we meet with an obscure indistinct welter of words, with current phrases, hackneyed expressions and fashionable locutions. Their nebulous productions consequently resemble printing with worn-out type.

With regard to the *tediousness* in writing touched on above, one should add the general observation that there are two kinds of tediousness: an objective and a subjective kind. The *objective* kind always derives from the deficiency in question, that is from the fact that the author has no clear ideas or information whatever to communicate. For he who has them goes about communicating them in a direct manner and consequently everywhere presents clear, distinct concepts, so that he is neither verbose, nor obscure, nor confused, and consequently he is not tedious. Even if his leading idea is false, it is in this event still clearly thought and well considered, that is to say at least formally correct, so that what he writes always retains some value. On the other hand, an objectively tedious work is, for the same reason, always worthless in every respect. – *Subjective* tediousness, on the contrary, is only relative: it originates in a lack of interest in the subject on the part of the reader; this, however, originates in the reader's limitations. The most admirable work, consequently, can be subjectively tedious, namely to this or that reader; as, conversely, the worst can be subjectively entertaining to this or that reader because the subject or the writer interests him.

An *affected* writer is like a man who dresses up so as not to be confused and confounded with the mob, a danger which a gentleman, however ill-clad, never runs. As a certain overdressing and *tiré à quatre épingles* thus betrays the plebeian, so an affected style betrays the commonplace mind.

Nevertheless, it is a misguided endeavour to try to write exactly as you speak. Every style of writing should rather retain a certain vestige of affinity with the lapidary style, which is indeed the ancestor of them all. This endeavour is consequently as objectionable as its converse, that is to try to speak as you write, which is at once pedantic and hard to understand.

Obscurity and vagueness of expression is always and everywhere a very bad sign: for in ninety-nine cases out of a hundred it derives from vagueness of thought, which in turn comes from an original incongruity and inconsistency in the thought itself, and thus from its falsity. If a true thought arises in a head it will immediately strive after clarity and will soon achieve it: what is clearly thought, however, easily finds the expression appropriate to it. The thoughts a man is capable of always express themselves in clear, comprehensible and unambiguous words. Those who put together difficult, obscure, involved, am-

biguous discourses do not really know what they want to say:
they have no more than a vague consciousness of it which is
only struggling towards a thought: often, however, they also
want to conceal from themselves and others that they actually
have nothing to say.

Truth is fairest naked, and the simpler its expression the profounder its influence. What declamation over the vanity of
human existence, for example, can well make a greater
impression than Job's: *Homo, natus de muliere, brevi vivit tem-
pore, repletus multis miseriis, qui, tanquam flos, egreditur et
conteritur, et fugit velut umbra.*[3] – It is for just this reason that
the naïve poetry of Goethe stands so incomparably higher than
the rhetorical poetry of Schiller. And it is this that accounts for
the powerful effect of many folk songs. Everything superfluous
is prejudicial.

More than nine-tenths of all literate men and women certainly read nothing but newspapers, and consequently model
their orthography, grammar and style almost exclusively on
them and even, in their simplicity, regard the murdering of language which goes on in them as brevity of expression, elegant
facility and ingenious innovation; indeed, young people of the
unlearned professions in general regard the newspaper as an
authority simply because it is something printed. For this
reason, the state should, in all seriousness, take measures to
ensure that the newspapers are altogether free of linguistic
errors. A censor should be instituted who, instead of receiving
a salary, should receive one louis d'or for every mangled or
stylistically objectionable word, error of grammar or syntax, or
misemployed preposition he discovers in them, and three louis
d'or for every instance of sheer impudent mockery of all style
and grammar, with double the sum for any repetition, the
amounts to be defrayed by the perpetrators. Or is the German

3. Job 14, 1–2: Man that is born of a woman is of few days, and full of
trouble. He cometh forth like a flower, and is cut down: he fleeth also as
a shadow, and continueth not.

language perhaps anyone's game, a trifle not worthy of that protection of the law which even a dunghill enjoys? – Miserable
philistines! – What in the world is to become of the German
language if every scribbler and newspaper writer is granted
discretionary power to do with it whatever his caprice and folly
suggest?

9

An error of style which, with literature in decline and the ancient
languages neglected, is becoming more and more common, but is
really at home only in Germany, is its *subjectivity*. It consists in
this, that the writer is satisfied so long as he himself understands
what he means: the reader may be left to make of it what he
can. Unconcerned with this difficulty, the writer proceeds as if
he were engaged in a monologue: while what should really be
taking place is a dialogue, and indeed one in which the speaker
has to express himself the more clearly in that he cannot hear
the listener's questions. It is for just this reason that a style
should be *not* subjective, but objective. An objective style is one
in which the words are so arranged that the reader is downright compelled to think exactly the same thing as the author
has thought. But this will come about only if the author continually remembers that thoughts obey the law of gravity to this
extent, that they travel much more easily from head down to
paper than they do from paper up to head, so that for the latter
journey they require all the assistance we can give them. If it is
achieved, the words operate in a purely objective way, like a
completed oil-painting; while the subjective style is hardly more
effective than a series of blots on a wall: only he whose imagination has chanced to be aroused by them can see in them
shapes and pictures – to others they are merely blots. The distinction in question applies to the whole mode of communication, but it can often be demonstrated in individual passages
too: for example, I have just read in a new book: 'I have not
written so as to increase the number of existing books.' This says
the opposite of what the writer intended, and is moreover nonsense.

10

He who writes carelessly makes first and foremost the confession that he himself does not place any great value on his thoughts. For the enthusiasm which inspires the unflagging endurance necessary for discovering the clearest, most forceful and most attractive form of expressing our thoughts is begotten only by the conviction of their weightiness and truth – just as we employ silver or golden caskets only for sacred things or priceless works of art.

11

Few write as an architect builds, drawing up a plan beforehand and thinking it out down to the smallest details. Most write as they play dominoes: their sentences are linked together as dominoes are, one by one, in part deliberately, in part by chance.

12

The guiding principle in the art of composition should be that the human being can think clearly only one thought at a time, so that he should not be asked to think two, not to speak of more than two thoughts at the same time. – But this is what he is being asked to do when parentheses are inserted into sentences which have been broken up to accommodate them, a practice which causes unnecessary and wanton confusion. *German* writers are the worst offenders in this respect. That their language lends itself to it more readily than other living languages may account for the fact but does not make it commendable. The prose of no language reads so pleasantly and easily as does that of the French, and this is because it is as a rule free of this error. The French writer sets his thoughts down one after the other in the most logical and natural order possible and thus places them before his reader in succession, so that the reader can give his undivided attention to each of them. The

German, on the other hand, weaves them together into an involved and twice involved and thrice involved period, because he insists on saying six things at once instead of presenting them one after the other.

The true national characteristic of the Germans is *ponderousness*:[4] it is evident in their gait, their activities, their language, their speech, their mode of narrating, their way of understanding and thinking, but especially in their *style of writing*, in the pleasure they take in long, ponderous, involved periods, where the memory has to bear the burden for a good five minutes, patient and unaided, until, at the end of the period, reason comes into action and the conundrum is solved. This is the kind of thing they enjoy, and if affectation and bombast can be introduced as well, the author revels in it: but Heaven help the reader.

It is obviously counter to all sound reason to clap one thought down straight over another, as if making a cross: but this is what happens when a writer interrupts what he has started to say in order to say something quite different in the middle of it, thus leaving a meaningless half-period in the custody of the reader until the other half comes along. It is like handing a guest an empty plate and leaving him to hope something will appear on it.

This form of construction reaches the height of tastelessness when the parentheses are not even dovetailed organically into the period but, by making a straight breach in it, simply wedged in. If it is an impertinence to interrupt others, it is no less of an impertinence to interrupt oneself, as happens in a form of construction which for some years now every inferior, careless, hasty scribbler with visions of payment before his eyes has employed six times on every page and enjoyed doing so. It consists – precept and example should, where possible, go together – in breaking off one phrase in order to stick another into it. They do it, however, not only from laziness, but also from stupidity, in

4. *Schwerfälligkeit*: heaviness, clumsiness, slowness, awkwardness, ponderousness.

that they take it for a pleasant *légèreté*[5] which enlivens the discourse. – In rare individual cases it may be excusable.

13

No literary quality – persuasiveness, for instance, or richness of imagery, a talent for metaphors, boldness, astringency, conciseness, gracefulness, facility of expression, wit, striking contrast, laconism, simplicity – can be acquired by reading writers who display it. But if we already possess any such quality as a natural tendency, that is *potentia*, we can by reading summon it up in ourselves, become conscious of it, see what can be made of it, be fortified in our inclination, indeed in the courage to employ it, judge of its effectiveness, and thus learn how to use it correctly: and only then shall we also possess it *actu*. This, then, is the only way in which reading can teach writing: it instructs us in the use we can make of our own natural gifts; thus it can instruct us only when we possess such gifts. If we do not possess them we can learn from reading nothing but cold dead mannerism, and become superficial imitators.

14

As the strata of the earth preserve in succession the living creatures of past epochs, so the shelves of libraries preserve in succession the errors of the past and their expositions, which like the former were very lively and made a great commotion in their own age but now stand petrified and stiff in a place where only the literary palaeontologist regards them.

15

According to Herodotus, Xerxes wept at the sight of his enormous army to think that, of all these men, not one would be alive in a hundred years' time; so who cannot but weep at the sight of the thick fair catalogue to think that, of all these books, not one will be alive in ten years' time.

5. Lightness of touch.

16

The art of *not* reading is a very important one. It consists in not taking an interest in whatever may be engaging the attention of the general public at any particular time. When some political or ecclesiastical pamphlet, or novel, or poem is making a great commotion, you should remember that he who writes for fools always finds a large public. – A precondition for reading good books is not reading bad ones: for life is short.

17

Buying books would be a good thing if one could also buy the time to read them in: but as a rule the purchase of books is mistaken for the appropriation of their contents.

18

In the history of the world half a century is a considerable period, because its material is always changing, inasmuch as something is always happening. In the history of literature, on the other hand, half a century is often no time at all, because nothing has happened: things are as they were fifty years before.

It is consistent with this state of things that we should see the scientific, literary and artistic *Zeitgeist* declared bankrupt about every thirty years: for during this period the errors contained in it have grown to such proportions as to crush it by the weight of their absurdity, while the opposing view has at the same time been strengthened by them. So now there is a sudden change: but what often succeeds is an error in the opposite direction. To exhibit the periodical recurrence of this state of things would be the true pragmatic material of literary history.

I wish someone would one day attempt a *tragic history of literature*, showing how the various nations which now take their highest pride in the great writers and artists they can show treated them while they were alive. In such a history, the author would bring visibly before us that endless struggle which the good and genuine of all ages and all lands has to endure against the always dominant bad and wrong-headed; depict the martyrdom of almost every genuine enlightener of mankind, almost every great master of every art; show us how, with a few exceptions, they lived tormented lives in poverty and wretchedness, without recognition, without sympathy, without disciples, while fame, honour and riches went to the unworthy; how, that is, their lot was that of Esau, who while out hunting and catching game for his father was robbed by Jacob of his father's blessing; but how, in spite of all, love of their cause sustained them, until the hard struggle of such an educator of the human race was at last consummated, the never-fading laurel-wreath beckoned and the hour struck in which for him too:

> *Der schwere Panzer wird zum Flügelkleide,*
> *Kurz ist der Schmerz, unendlich ist die Freude.*[6]

6. The heavy armour becomes the light dress of childhood; the pain is brief, the joy unending.

ON VARIOUS SUBJECTS

I

A

INSTEAD of trying to show that the works of nature and of the art-impulse demonstrate the wisdom of God, as the English do, one should learn from them that everything which comes about through the medium of the *idea*, that is to say of the intellect, even though this intellect has advanced to the point of attaining reason, is mere bungling compared with what proceeds directly from the will as thing in itself and is not communicated through an idea, of which the works of nature are an instance. This is the theme of my essay *On the Will in Nature*.

B

Among people untrained in philosophy – which includes all who have not studied the philosophy of Kant, that is to say most foreigners – and no less among many present-day physicians, etc., in Germany who are content to philosophize on the basis of their catechism, there still exists the old, fundamentally false antithesis between *mind and matter*. – From this false antithesis there arise Spiritualists and Materialists. The latter assert that matter, through its form and composition, produces everything, consequently produces thought and will in man; which view the former cry out against. In reality, however, although there are certainly many nonsensical ideas and chimeras, there is neither mind nor matter in the world. The exertion of weight in a stone is every bit as inexplicable as is thought in a human brain: this fact would suggest the presence of a mind in the stone. For this reason I would say to these disputants: you believe you perceive dead, i.e. completely passive material void of all qualities, because you suppose you can truly understand everything which you are able to trace back to a *mechanistic* effect. But as physical and chemical effects are avowedly incomprehensible to you so long as you cannot trace them back to mechanistic effects, so are these mechanistic effects themselves – that is to say, modes of expression proceeding from weight, impenetrability, cohesion, hardness, inflexibility, elasticity, fluidity, etc. – just as mysterious as these others, indeed as mysterious as thought in the human head. If matter can (you know not why) fall to earth, so it can also (you know not why) think. What is really comprehensible through and through in mechanics extends no further in any account of an effect than what is purely mathematical; it is limited, that is to say, to determining its spatial and temporal qualities. Both of these, however, together with all the laws which govern them, are known to us *a priori,* and are consequently no more than the forms of our knowledge and belong exclusively to the realm of ideas. What determines them is thus at bottom subjective: it does not involve the purely objective, that which is independent of our knowledge of it, the thing in itself. Even in mechanics, as soon as we go beyond what is purely mathematical, as soon as we arrive at impenetrability, at weight, at inflexibility, or fluidity, or gaseity, we stand before modes of expression which are just as mysterious to us as the thought and will of man, that is to say before the directly unfathomable: for unfathomable is what every natural force is. But where now is *matter*, which you know and understand so intimately that you intend to explain everything by it, trace everything back to it? – Now if you suppose the existence of a *mind* in the human head, as a *deus ex machina*, then, as already remarked, you are bound to concede a mind to every stone. If, on the other hand, your dead and purely passive *matter* can, as weight, exert itself, or as electricity attract, repel and give off sparks, then it can also, as grey-matter, think. In short: all ostensible mind can be attributed to matter, but all matter can likewise be attributed to mind; from which it follows that the antithesis is a false one.

C

No science impresses the masses more than *astronomy*. The almost idolatrous veneration in which *Newton* is held, especially in England, passes belief. Only a little while ago *The Times* called him 'the greatest of human beings', and in 1815 (according to a report in the *Examiner*) one of Newton's teeth was sold for 750 pounds sterling to a Lord who had it mounted on a ring. Now this ludicrous degree of veneration accorded the great master of arithmetic comes from the fact that people take as the measure of his deserts the magnitude of the masses the laws of whose motions he determined and traced back to the natural force causing them (which last was in any case not his discovery but that of *Robert Hooke*:[1] he merely confirmed it by arithmetic). For otherwise it is impossible to see why more honour should be due to him than anyone else who traces a given effect back to the expression of a certain natural force, or why *Lavoisier*,[2] for example, should not be rated just as highly. To explain given phenomena as the combined action of various different natural forces, and even to discover these forces only as a result of this explanation, is on the contrary a far harder task than that which has to consider only two, and two such simply and uniformly acting forces as gravitation and inertia in unresisting space. It is on precisely this unexampled simplicity, or poverty, of its material that the mathematical certainty and exactitude of astronomy rests by virtue of which it astonishes the world by being able even to announce the existence of planets no one has ever seen. This last achievement, though it be never so greatly admired, is, regarded in the cold light of day, no more than the identical act of reasoning which is undertaken when any still invisible cause is determined from the effects it manifests, and which was performed to an even more wonderful degree by that connoisseur who knew with certainty from a

1. Robert Hooke (1635–1703), physicist. 'He was the first to state clearly that the motions of the heavenly bodies must be regarded as mechanical problems.' (*Encyclopaedia Britannica*)

2. Antoine Laurent Lavoisier (1743–94), 'the father of modern chemistry'.

single glass of wine that there must be leather in the barrel, which was denied until, when the barrel was at length empty, a key with a little strap attached to it was found at the bottom. The act of reasoning here is the same as that involved in the discovery of Neptune, and the difference lies merely in its application, that is to say in the object to which it is addressed; it differs in its material, not at all in its form.

D

The polemicizing against the assumption of a *life force* which is now becoming fashionable deserves to be called not so much mistaken as downright stupid. For whoever denies the life force is fundamentally denying his own existence, and may thus boast of having scaled the topmost peak of absurdity. In so far as this impudent nonsense proceeds from physicians and chemists, however, it also involves the basest ingratitude: for the life force is what overcomes sickness and produces the cures for which these gentlemen subsequently pocket the money. – If there exists no natural force whose essential property is just as much to act *purposefully* as it is the essential property of gravity to keep physical bodies together, which moves, directs and orders the entire complex workings of the organism, and which expresses itself in it in the same way as gravity expresses itself in the phenomenon of falling, then life is only a semblance, an illusion, and every creature is in reality a mere automaton, i.e. a play of mechanical, physical and chemical forces. – Physical and chemical forces *are* active in the animal organism, to be sure: but that which holds them together and directs them, so that they constitute a purposive and enduring organism, is the life force. To believe that physical and chemical forces could by themselves bring about an organism is not merely mistaken but, as already remarked, stupid. – This life force is in itself will.

The life force is actually identical with the will, so that what appears to the self-consciousness as will is in unconscious, organic life that *primum mobile* which has very fittingly been called the life force. It is from a simple analogy with this that we conclude that the other natural forces are fundamentally identical with will, only in these forces the will stands at a lower stage of objectivization.

E

I say in my principal work: 'The genitals are, far more than any other external member of the body, subject entirely to the will and not at all to knowledge: indeed the will shows itself almost as independent of knowledge here as it does in those parts which, responding merely to stimuli, serve to propagate vegetative life.' [3] In fact, *ideas* do not act on the genitals in the form of *motivation*, as they do on the will in every other case, but, because the erection is a reflex action, merely in the form of stimulus, and therefore directly and only so long as they are *present*: another requirement if they are to be efficacious is that they must be present for a certain length of time, whereas an idea which acts in the form of motivation often does so in the very briefest time and its efficacy has in general no relation to the duration of its presence. Further: the effect which an idea has on the genitals cannot, like that of a motivation, be *annulled* by another idea, except in so far as the second idea *suppresses* consciousness of the first, so that the first is no longer *present*: but in that event the effect is unfailingly annulled, even when the second idea contains nothing contrary to the first, which is what is required of a counter-motivation. – It is accordingly not sufficient for the accomplishment of coitus that the presence of a woman should act on the man in the form of a motivation (the production of children, for example, or the performance of duty), however powerful this motivation may be in itself; her presence must act in the form of direct *stimulus*.

F

I very much hold to the view that acute illnesses are, with a few exceptions, nothing other than curative processes instituted by

3. *The World as Will and Idea*, vol. 1, section 60.

nature itself to remedy some disorder in the organism; to which end the *vis naturae medicatrix*, invested with dictatorial powers, has recourse to extraordinary measures, and these constitute the illness we feel. The simplest *type* of this general procedure is provided by the common cold. When we get cold the activity of the outer skin is paralysed and excretion by exhalation is thereby prevented, which could lead to our death. But when this happens the inner skin, the mucous membrane, takes over the task of the outer: and this constitutes a common cold, an illness, yet clearly no more than a process for curing the actual but not perceptible illness, the cessation of the functioning of the skin. This illness, the common cold, then passes through the same stages as the primary illness: onset, intensification, climax and decline; at first acute, it gradually grows chronic and remains in this state until the fundamental but not perceptible trouble, the paralysis of the skin-function, is over. It is therefore mortally dangerous to suppress a cold. An identical procedure constitutes the essence of almost all illnesses, and these are in reality only the medicine of the *vis naturae medicatrix*.

2

My chief objection to pantheism is that it signifies nothing. To call the world God is not to explain it but merely to enrich the language with a superfluous synonym for the word world. It comes to the same thing whether you say 'the world is God' or 'the world is the world'. If you started from God as that which is given and to be explained, and said 'God is the world', then, to be sure, you would be offering some kind of explanation, inasmuch as it would trace *ignotus* back to *notius*, but still no more than an explanation of a word. But if you start from what actually is given, the world, and say 'the world is God', then it is as plain as day that this says nothing, or at the most explains *ignotum per ignotius*.

It follows that pantheism presupposes the pre-existence of theism: for only by starting from a God, that is to say by already having one and being familiar with him, can you finally come to identify him with the world, actually in order politely to set him aside. You do not start, unprejudiced, from the world as that which is to be explained, you start from God as that which is given, but, soon not knowing what to do with him, you let the world take over his role. That is the origin of pantheism. For it would never occur to anyone taking an unprejudiced view of the world to regard it as a God. It would clearly have to be a very ill-advised God who knew of nothing better to do than to transform himself into a world such as this one.

The great advance which pantheism is supposed to represent over theism is, if taken seriously and not as a mere disguised negation, a transition from the unproved and hardly conceivable to the downright absurd. For however obscure, vague and confused the concept may be which is attached to the word God, two predicates are nonetheless inseparable from it: supreme power and supreme wisdom. But that a being equipped with these should have transplanted himself into a situation such as this world represents is frankly an absurd idea: for our situation in the world is obviously one into which no intelligent, not to speak of all-wise being would transplant himself.

3

A

In the first broad outlines of the Greek system of gods one can glimpse an allegorical representation of the highest ontological and cosmological principles. – Uranus is *space*, the first condition for all existence, thus the first begetter. Cronus is *time*. He castrates the procreative principle: time annihilates all generative power; or more precisely: the capacity for generating *new forms*, the primary generation of living races, ends after the first world-period. Zeus, who is rescued from the voraciousness of his father, is *matter*: it alone escapes the power of time, which destroys everything else: it persists. From matter, however, all other things proceed: Zeus is the father of gods and men.

B

The continuity, indeed the unity of human with animal and all other nature, thus that of the microcosmos with the macrocosmos, is expressed by the mysterious, enigmatic Sphinx, by the centaurs, by Ephesian Artemis with diverse animal forms disposed beneath her countless breasts, as it is by the Egyptian human bodies with animal heads and the Indian Gawesa, and finally by the Ninevite bulls and lions with human heads, which recall the avatar as man-lion.

C

The sons of Iapetus represent four basic qualities of the human character, together with the suffering which comes with them. *Atlas*, the patient, has to bear and endure. *Menoetius*, the brave, is overpowered and hurled to destruction. *Prometheus*, the wise and prudent, is bound, i.e. his effectiveness is limited [4] and a vulture, i.e. care, gnaws at his heart. *Epimetheus*, the rash and thoughtless, is punished by his own folly.

D

I have always found the legend of *Pandora* incomprehensible, indeed preposterous and absurd. I suspect that Hesiod himself already misunderstood it and distorted its meaning. It is not all the evil but all the good things of the world which Pandora had in her box (as her name already indicates). When Epimetheus rashly opened it the good things flew out and away: Hope alone was saved and still remains with us.

4. *In seiner Wirksamkeit gehemmt*: curbed in his efficacy – an odd locution which must, I think, derive from Prometheus's words in Goethe's dramatic fragment: asked by Epimetheus how much he possesses, he replies: '*Der Kreis, den meine Wirksamkeit erfüllt*!' – 'The circle within which my effectiveness extends! (*or* My sphere of influence!) – Nothing less and nothing more!'

E

It is not without meaning that mythology depicts Cronus as devouring and digesting stones: for that which is otherwise quite indigestible, all affliction, vexation, loss, grief, time alone digests.

F

The downfall of the Titans, whom Zeus hurls into the underworld, seems to be the same story as the downfall of the angels who rebelled against Jehovah.

The story of Idomeneus, who sacrificed his son *ex voto*, and that of Jephtha is essentially the same.

Can it be that, as the root of the Gothic and the Greek languages lies in Sanskrit, so there is an older mythology from which the Greek and the Jewish mythologies derive? If you cared to give scope to your imagination you could even adduce that the twofold-long night in which Zeus begot Heracles on Alcmene came about because further east Joshua at Jericho told the sun to stand still. Zeus and Jehovah were thus assisting one another: for the gods of Heaven are, like those of earth, always secretly in alliance. But how innocent was the pastime of Father Zeus compared with the bloodthirsty activities of Jehovah and his chosen brigands.

G

Viewed from the summit of my philosophy, which, as is well known, is the standpoint of asceticism, the *affirmation of the will to live* is concentrated in the act of procreation and this is its most resolute expression. Now the meaning of this affirmation is intrinsically this, that the will, which is originally without knowledge and thus a blind impulse, arrives at knowledge of its own nature through the world as idea but does not allow itself to be distracted or checked in its desire and passion by this knowledge; it henceforth desires consciously and with full awareness that which it formerly desired as a knowledgeless drive and impulse. In accordance with this, we find that he who ascetically *denies* life through voluntary chastity differs empirically from him who affirms life through acts of procreation in that what takes place without knowledge as a blind physiological function, namely in sleep, in the case of the former, in the case of the latter is carried out with conscious awareness, and thus takes place in the light of knowledge. Now it is in fact very remarkable that this abstract philosophical dictum, which is by no means allied to the spirit of the Greeks, should, together with the empirical events which confirm it, possess an exact allegorical representation in the beautiful legend of *Psyche*, who was permitted to enjoy Amor only if she did not see him but who, ignoring every warning, nonetheless insisted on seeing him, whereupon, in accordance with the ineluctable decree of mysterious powers, she was plunged into limitless misery, which she could emerge from only after a sojourn in the underworld and the performance of heavy tasks there.

4

History, which I like to think of as the antithesis of poetry, is in relation to time what geography is in relation to space. The former is, no more than the latter, a science in the true sense of the term: they both have for their subject-matter, not universal truths, but only individual things. History has always been a favourite study of those who want to learn something without being put to the effort demanded by the true sciences, which require the exercise of reason; but in our own time it is more popular than ever before, as is demonstrated by the countless history books which appear every year. Since I cannot avoid seeing in all history nothing but a repetition of the same things, as when a kaleidoscope is turned you see only the same things in differing configurations, I cannot share this passionate interest, though I do not go on to censure it: my only objection is that many want to make history a department of philosophy, indeed to identify it with philosophy, in that they believe it can be substituted for it, and this is ludicrous and absurd. An illustration of the preference which the general public has always had for history is provided by social conversation as usually conducted: it consists as a rule in this, that one person narrates something and then another person narrates something else, under which condition everyone is certain of his share of attention. As here, so in history we see the mind occupied with quite individual things for their own sake.

On the other hand, history might be regarded as a continuation of zoology, inasmuch as, while in the case of the animals it is sufficient to consider the species, in the case of man, who has individual character, we have to familiarize ourselves with individuals too, together with the individual events which condition them. The essential incompleteness of history is a direct consequence of this fact, because individuals and events are innumerable and without end. With the study of history, what you have learned in no way reduces the sum of what you have still to learn: with all true sciences, a complete knowledge is at any rate conceivable. – When the history of China and India stand open to us, the endlessness of the material thus revealed will make plain the absurdity of this course and will compel those who are avid for this kind of knowledge to see that you have to recognize the many in the one, the rule in the individual case, the ways of nations in the knowledge of human actions, but not reckon up facts *ad infinitum*.

To the essential incompleteness of history referred to above must be added the fact that Clio, the Muse of History, is as thoroughly infected with lies as a streetwalker is with syphilis. It is my belief that the events and characters narrated by history compare with reality more or less as the portraits of authors on frontispieces of books usually compare with the authors themselves, that is to say they do so only in outline, so that they bear only a faint similarity to them, or sometimes none at all.

Newspapers are the second hand [5] of history. This hand, however, is usually not only of inferior metal to the other two hands, it also seldom works properly. The so-called 'leading articles' in

5. I.e. hand indicating seconds on clock.

them are the chorus to the drama of current events. Exaggeration in every sense is as essential to newspaper writing as it is to the writing of plays: for the point is to make as much as possible of every occurrence. So that all newspaper writers are, for the sake of their trade, alarmists: this is their way of making themselves interesting. What they really do, however, is resemble little dogs who, as soon as anything whatever moves, start up a loud barking. It is necessary, therefore, not to pay too much attention to their alarms, and to realize in general that the newspaper is a magnifying glass, and this only at best: for very often it is no more than a shadow-play on the wall.

As every man possesses a physiognomy by which you can provisionally judge him, so every age also possesses one that is no less characteristic. For the *Zeitgeist* of every age is like a sharp east wind which blows through everything. You can find traces of it in all that is done, thought and written, in music and painting, in the flourishing of this or that art: it leaves its mark on everything and everyone, so that, e.g., an age of phrases without meaning must also be one of music without melody and form without aim or object. Thus the spirit of an age also bestows on it its outward physiognomy. The ground-bass to this is always played by architecture: its pattern is followed first of all by ornaments, vessels, furniture and utensils of all kinds, and finally even by clothes, together with the manner in which the hair and beard are cut.[6]

5

A

To estimate a *genius* you should not take the mistakes in his productions, or his weaker works, but only those works in which he excels. For even in the realm of the intellect, weakness and absurdity cleave so firmly to human nature that even the most brilliant mind is not always entirely free of them: whence the

6. The beard, being a half-mask, should be forbidden by the police. It is, moreover, as a sexual symbol in the middle of the face, *obscene*: that is why it pleases women. [*Schopenhauer's note.*]

mighty errors which can be pointed to even in the works of the greatest men, and hence Horace's *Quandoque bonus dormitat Homerus*. What distinguishes genius, on the other hand, and provides a measure for estimating it, is the height to which it was able to rise when time and mood were propitious and which remains for ever unachievable to ordinary talents.

B

The great misfortune for intellectual merit is that it has to wait until the good is praised by those who produce only the bad; indeed, the misfortune already lies in the general fact that it has to receive its crown from the hands of human judgement, a quality of which most people possess about as much as a castrate possesses of the power to beget children.

Power of discrimination, *esprit de discernement*, and consequently judgement: that is what is lacking. They do not know how to distinguish the genuine from the spurious, the wheat from the chaff, gold from tin, and they do not perceive the great distance which separates the commonplace herd from the very rarest. The result is the state of things expressed by the ancient couplet:

> *Es ist nun das Geschick der Grossen hier auf Erden,*
> *Erst wann sie nicht mehr sind, von uns erkannt zu werden.*[7]

This lamentable lack of the power to discriminate is no less evident in the sciences, namely in the tenacious life of false and refuted theories. Once come into general credit, they continue to defy truth for centuries. After a hundred years Copernicus had not yet supplanted Ptolemy. Bacon, Descartes, Locke prevailed very slowly and very late. It was no different with Newton: you have only to see the animosity and mockery with which Leibniz opposed the Newtonian gravitational system in his controversy with Clarke. Although Newton lived for almost forty

7. It is the fate of the great here on earth to be recognized by us only when they are no more.

years after the appearance of his *Principia*, his theory was, when he died, recognized only in England, and there only partially, while abroad he could, according to the preface to Voltaire's account of his theory, count fewer than twenty adherents. On the other hand, in our own day Newton's absurd theory of colours still holds the field, forty years after the appearance of Goethe's.[8] Hume, although he started publishing very early and wrote in a thoroughly popular style, was disregarded until his fiftieth year.[9] Kant, although he wrote and taught his whole life long, became famous only after his sixtieth year. – Artists and poets have a better chance than thinkers, to be sure, because their public is at least a hundred times bigger: and yet what did Mozart and Beethoven count for during their lifetime? or Dante, or even Shakespeare? If the contemporaries of this last had had any idea of his worth, that blossoming time of painting would have given us at any rate *one* good, well attested portrait of him, whereas all we have are a number of altogether doubtful paintings, a very bad engraving and an even worse funeral monument bust. We would likewise possess hundreds of his manuscripts instead of merely a couple of legal signatures. – Every Portuguese is proud of Camoens,[10] the only Portuguese poet: but he lived on alms procured for him in the streets every evening by a Negro boy he had brought back from India.

c

As the sun needs an eye in order to shine, and music an ear in order to sound, so the worth of every masterpiece in art and science is conditioned by the mind related and equal to it to which it speaks. Only such a mind possesses the incantation to arouse the spirits imprisoned in such a work and make them show themselves. The commonplace head stands before it as be-

8. See Introduction, p. 37.

9. David Hume (1711–76), the foremost British philosopher of the eighteenth century.

10. Luis Vaz de Camoes (English form Camoens) (1524–80), not literally the only Portuguese poet but the only one whose reputation extends outside Portugal.

fore a magic casket he cannot open, or before an instrument he cannot play and from which he can therefore summon only inchoate noises, however much he would like to deceive himself in the matter. A beautiful work requires a sensitive mind, a speculative work a thinking mind, in order really to exist and to live.

D

Great minds are related to the brief span of time during which they live as great buildings are to a little square in which they stand: you cannot see them in all their magnitude because you are standing too close to them.

6

A

When you see the many and manifold institutions for teaching and learning and the great crowd of pupils and masters which throngs them you might think the human race was much occupied with wisdom and insight. But here too appearance is deceptive. The latter teach to earn money, and strive not for wisdom but for the appearance of it and to be credited with it; the former learn, not to achieve knowledge and insight, but so as to be able to chatter about them and give themselves airs. Every thirty years a new generation appears which knows nothing and then sets about trying to gulp down summarily and as fast as possible all the human knowledge assembled over the millennia, after which it would like to think it knows more than all the past put together. To this end it resorts to universities and reaches out for books, and for the most recent ones too, as being its own contemporaries and fellows of its own age. Everything quick and everything new! as new as it itself is. And then off it goes, loud with its own opinions!

B

Students and learned men of every kind and every age go as a rule in search of *information*, not *insight*. They make it a point of honour to have information about everything: it does not occur to them that information is merely a *means* towards insight and possesses little or no value in itself. When I see how much these well-informed people know, I sometimes say to myself: Oh, how little such a one must have had to think about, since he has had so much time for reading!

C

The completest erudition compares with genius as a herbarium compares with the ever self-renewing, ever fresh, ever youthful, ever changing plant-world, and there is no greater contrast than that between the erudition of the commentator and the childlike *naïveté* of the ancient author.

D

Dilettantes! Dilettantes! – this is the derogatory cry those who apply themselves to art or science for the sake of gain raise against those who pursue it for love of it and pleasure in it. This derogation rests on their vulgar conviction that no one would take up a thing seriously unless prompted to it by want, hunger, or some other kind of greediness. The public has the same outlook and consequently holds the same opinion, which is the origin of its universal respect for 'the professional' and its mistrust of the dilettante. The truth, however, is that to the dilettante the thing is the end, while to the professional as such it is the means; and only he who is directly interested in a thing, and occupies himself with it from love of it, will pursue it with entire seriousness. It is from such as these, and not from wage-earners, that the greatest things have always come.

E

The abolition of Latin as the universal learned language, and the introduction in its place of the parochialism of national literatures, has been a real misfortune for science and learning in Europe, in the first place because it was only through the medium of the Latin language that a universal European learned public existed at all, to the totality of which every book that appeared directed itself; and in all Europe the number of heads capable of thinking and forming judgements is moreover already so small that if their forum is broken up and kept asunder by language barriers their beneficial effect is infinitely weakened. To this great disadvantage, however, a second, even worse one will soon be added: the classical languages will soon cease to be taught. Neglect of them is already getting the upper hand in France and even in Germany. That as early as the 1830s the *Corpus juris* was translated into German was an unmistakable sign that ignorance of the basis of all learning, the Latin language, had entered upon the scene, that is to say barbarism had entered upon the scene. It has now got to the point at which Greek and even Latin authors are published in editions with *German* notes, which is beastliness and an infamy. The real reason (whatever the gentlemen may say) is that the editors no longer know how to write Latin, and our dear young people are only too glad to follow them along the paths of laziness, ignorance and barbarism.

A vile practice appearing with more impudent blatantness every day which deserves special reproof is that in scholarly books and in specifically learned journals, even those published by academies, passages from Greek, and even (*proh pudor*) from Latin authors are cited in German translation. Devil take it! Are you writing for tailors and cobblers?

If this is what it has come to, then farewell humanity, noble taste and cultivation! Barbarism is returning, despite railways, electricity and flying balloons. We are finally losing another advantage enjoyed by all our forefathers: it is not only Roman antiquity which Latin preserves for us, it is equally the entire Middle Ages of every European land and modern times down to the middle of the last century. Scotus Erigena from the ninth century, John of Salisbury from the twelfth, Raymond Lully from the thirteenth, together with a hundred others, speak to me directly in the language natural and proper to them as soon as they began thinking on scholarly subjects: they still approach close up to me, I am in direct contact with them and learn to know them truly. What would it be if each had written in the language of his own country as it was in his time? I I wouldn't understand as much as half of it, and real intellectual contact with them would be impossible: I would see them as silhouettes on the distant horizon or, worse, through the telescope of a translation. It was to guard against this that Bacon, as he expressly says, himself translated his own essays into Latin under the title *Sermones fideles* – in which, however, he had the assistance of Hobbes.

It should here be remarked in passing that patriotism, when it wants to make itself felt in the domain of learning, is a dirty fellow who should be thrown out of doors. For what could be more impertinent than, where the purely and universally human is the only concern, and where truth, clarity and beauty should alone be of any account, to presume to put into the scales one's preference for the country to which one's own valued person happens to belong, and then, with that in view, do violence to truth and commit injustice against the great minds of other nations in order to puff up the lesser minds of one's own?

7

In accordance with the nature of our intellect, *concepts* ought to arise through abstraction from our *perceptions*, consequently perception should precede concept. If this has in fact happened, as it has in the case of the man whose own experience is his only book and teacher, then he knows quite well what perceptions belong to which of his concepts and are represented by them. We may call this 'natural education'.

In the case of artificial education, on the contrary, the head is, through lectures, teaching and reading, stuffed full of concepts before there is any wide acquaintanceship with the perceptual world at all. Experience is then supposed to supply the perceptions to fit these concepts: up to that time, however, they have been wrongly applied, and things and men consequently wrongly judged, wrongly seen, wrongly dealt with. So it happens that education produces wrong-headedness, and that is why in youth, after much reading and learning, we go out into the world in part naïve, in part confused, and conduct ourselves in it now with arrogance, now with timidity: our heads are full of concepts which we are now endeavouring to apply, but which we almost always apply wrongly.

B

In accordance with the foregoing, the chief factor in education would be that *acquaintanceship with the world*, the achievement of which we may designate the object of all education, should *begin from the right end*. This, however, depends, as has been shown, on *perception* always preceding *concept*, and further on the narrower concept preceding the wider, and the entire course of instruction thus proceeding in the order in which concepts *presuppose* one another. As soon, however, as something in this series is overleaped, there arise defective concepts, and from these false concepts, and finally a wrong-headed view of the world, of which almost everyone carries his own version around in his head, some for a long time, most for ever. Correct understanding of many quite simple things comes only when one is advanced in years, and sometimes it then comes suddenly: there has been as it were a blind spot in one's acquaintanceship with the world, originating in an overleaping of the subject in one's early education, whether this education was an artificial one or a natural one through one's own experience.

C

Because errors imbibed early are mostly ineradicable and because the reasoning faculty is the last to mature, children should not, until they are sixteen, be exposed to any subject in which major errors are possible, that is to say philosophy, religion and general views of all kinds; they should be introduced only to those in which error is either impossible, as in mathematics, or of no great moment, as in languages, natural science, history, etc., in general however only to such studies as are accessible to their age and completely comprehensible. Childhood and youth is the time for assembling data and for becoming specifically and thoroughly acquainted with individual things; reasoning and judgement in general must remain in suspense and ultimate explanations be deferred. Since the reasoning faculty presupposes maturity and experience, it should be let alone for the time being: the impression of prejudices upon it before it is mature will damage it for good.

D

Maturity of knowledge, i.e. the degree of perfection to which knowledge can attain in each individual, consists in this, that in every case an exact correspondence has been achieved between abstract concept and perceptual comprehension, so that every concept rests directly or indirectly on a perceptual basis, through which alone it possesses real value, and that every perception can likewise be subsumed under the concept appropriate to it. Maturity is solely the work of experience and consequently of time. For, since we usually acquire our perceptual and our abstract knowledge separately, the former by natural means, the latter through good or bad instruction and communication from others, there is in youth usually little correspondence between our concepts, which have been fixed by mere words, and the real knowledge we have acquired through perception. These approach one another only gradually and mutually correct one another: but only when they are entirely united is our knowledge mature.

8

The animal voice serves only to express excitement and agitation of the *will*; the human, however, serves also to express *knowledge*; this is consistent with the fact that the former almost always makes an unpleasant impression on us, the voices of a few birds alone excepted.

When human language began to evolve, the beginning was certainly made by *interjections*, which express not concepts but, like the sounds made by animals, feelings, agitations of the will. The differences between them soon made themselves felt, and out of this difference there arose the transition to substantives, verbs, personal pronouns, etc.

The word of man is the most durable of all material. Once a poet has embodied his fleeting sensations in words appropriate to them, they live on in those words through the millennia and stir anew in every receptive reader.

9

That the outer mirrors the inner, and that the countenance expresses and reveals the whole essence of a man, is a presupposition whose a-priority and consequent certainty is manifested in the universal desire to *see* any man who has made himself prominent in any way, whether for good deeds or bad, or who has produced some extraordinary work; or, if this proves impossible, to learn from others *what he looks like*. Likewise, in everyday life, everyone inspects the face of anyone he meets and silently tries to discover in advance from his physiognomy his moral and intellectual nature. None of this would be so if, as some fools believe, a man's appearance possessed no significance and the body bore no closer relation to the soul than the coat does to the body.

The contrary is the case: every human face is a hieroglyph which can be deciphered, indeed whose key we bear ready-made within us. It is even true that a man's face as a rule says more, and more interesting things than his mouth, for it is a compendium of everything his mouth will ever say, in that it is the monogram of all this man's thoughts and aspirations. The mouth, further, expresses only the thoughts of a man, while the face expresses a thought of nature: so that everyone is worth looking at, even if everyone is not worth talking to.

We all proceed on the basis of the unspoken rule that every

man *is* as he *looks*: this is a correct rule; the difficulty lies in applying it. The capacity for doing so is in part inborn, in part to be gained through experience, but no one ever perfects it: even the most practised detect errors in themselves. Yet the face does not lie: it is we who read what is not written there. In any event, the deciphering of the face is a great and difficult art. Its principles can never be learned *in abstracto*. The first precondition for practising it is that you must take a *purely objective* view of your man, which is not so easy to do: for as soon as the slightest trace of aversion, or partiality, or fear, or hope, or even the thought of what impression we ourselves are making on *him*, in short as soon as anything subjective is involved, the hieroglyph becomes confused and corrupted. Just as we can hear the sound of a language only if we do not understand it, because otherwise what is signified at once suppresses consciousness of the sign which signifies it, so we can see the physiognomy of a man only if he is a stranger to us: consequently one can, strictly speaking, receive a purely objective impression of a face, and thus have the possibility of deciphering it, only at first sight.

Let us not dissemble over the fact that this first sight is usually extremely disagreeable. With the exception of the beautiful, good-natured or intelligent faces – with the exception, that is, of a very few, rare faces – I believe that every new face will usually arouse in a person of finer feeling a sensation akin to terror, since it presents the disagreeable in a new and surprising combination. As a rule it is in truth a sorry sight.[11] There are even some upon whose face there is imprinted such naïve vulgarity and lowness of character combined with such beast-like narrowness of mind that one wonders why they go around with such a face and do not rather wear a mask. Indeed, there are faces at the mere sight of which one feels polluted. – The *metaphysical* explanation of this fact would involve the consideration that the individuality of each man is precisely that of which, through his existence itself, he is to be cured. If, on the other hand, you are content with the *psychological* explanation,

11. The last three words in English in the original.

you should ask yourself what kind of physiognomy is to be expected of those in whom in the course of a long life there has very rarely arisen anything but petty, base, miserable thoughts and common, selfish, base and mischievous desires. Each of them, while it was present, set its mark on his face, and by much repetition deeply engraved itself there.

10

Kant wrote an essay on the *vital powers*: I should prefer to write a dirge and threnody on them, because their continual employment in banging and hammering and general noise-making has been a daily torment to me all my life. There are people, I know, indeed very many of them, who smile at these things, because they are insensitive to noise; but these are the same people who are insensitive to argument, to ideas, to poetry and works of art, in short to intellectual impressions of every kind, the reason being the tough constitution and firm texture of their brain. On the other hand, I have discovered complaints about the torment noise causes thinking men in the biographies or other personal statements of almost all the great writers, e.g. in Kant's, in Goethe's, in Lichtenberg's, in Jean Paul's; indeed, if such a complaint is missing, it is merely because the context failed to provide an opportunity for it. I explain the matter as follows: as when a large diamond is broken to pieces its value is equal to only so many little diamonds, or when an army is reduced to small units it becomes ineffective, so when a great mind is interrupted, disturbed and distracted it is capable of no more than a commonplace mind, because its superiority consists in concentrating all its forces on *one* single point and object, in the same way as a concave mirror concentrates all its rays, and this is precisely what noisy interruption prevents it from doing. That is why eminent minds have always been so extremely averse to every kind of disturbance, interruption and distraction, and most of all to violent interruption by noise, while the rest are not especially troubled by it. The most sensible and intelligent of all European nations has even called the rule

'Never interrupt' [12] the Eleventh Commandment. Noise, however, is the most impertinent of all interruptions, since it interrupts, indeed disrupts, even our thoughts. Where there is nothing to interrupt, to be sure, it will cause no especial discomfiture.

II

A

Two Chinamen visiting Europe went to the theatre for the first time. One of them occupied himself with trying to understand the theatrical machinery, which he succeeded in doing. The other, despite his ignorance of the language, sought to unravel the meaning of the play. The former is like the astronomer, the latter the philosopher.

B

No rose without a thorn. But many a thorn without a rose.

C

The dog is rightly the symbol of loyalty: in the plant-world, however, it should be the fir-tree. For it alone abides with us through bad times as well as good; it does not desert us when the sun does, like all other trees, plants, birds and insects – to return only when the sky above us is blue again.

D

A mother had, for their education and betterment, given her children Aesop's fables to read. Very soon, however, they brought the book back to her, and the eldest, who was very knowing and precocious, said: 'This is not a book for us! It's much too childish and silly. We've got past believing that foxes, wolves and ravens can talk: we're far too grown-up for such nonsense!' – Who cannot see in this hopeful lad the future enlightened Rationalist?

12. In English in the original.

E

Once when I was collecting specimens under an oak-tree I found, among the other plants and weeds, and of the same size as they, a plant of a dark colour with contracted leaves and a straight, rigid stalk. When I made to touch it, it said in a firm voice: 'Let me alone! I am no weed for your herbarium, like these others to whom nature has given a bare year of life. My life is measured in centuries: I am a little oak-tree.' – Thus does he whose influence is to be felt across the centuries stand, as a child, as a youth, often still as a man, indeed as a living creature as such, apparently like the rest and as insignificant as they. But just give him time and, with time, those who know how to recognize him. He will not die like the rest.

LIST OF CORRESPONDENCES

The present selection of Schopenhauer's *Essays and Aphorisms* is taken from *Parerga und Paralipomena. Kleine philosophische Schriften. Zweiter Band: Vereinzelte, jedoch systematisch geordnete Gedanken über vielerlei Gegenstände*, in the edition of Eduard Grisebach. In the following list of correspondences the first number is that of the section in the present selection, the second that of the same section in the original. Most sections are abridged.

On the Suffering of the World 1:148, 2:149, 3:150, 4:151, 5:152, 6:153, 7:154, 8:155, 9:156 (Kap. XII: Nachträge zur Lehre vom Leiden der Welt).

On the Vanity of Existence 1:142, 2:143, 3:144, 4:145, 5:146, 6:147 (Kap. XI: Nachträge zur Lehre von der Nichtigkeit des Daseyns).

On the Antithesis of Thing in Itself and Appearance 1:61, 2:62, 3:63, 4:65, 5:67 (Kap. IV: Einige Betrachtungen über den Gegensatz des Dinges an sich und der Erscheinung).

On Affirmation and Denial of the Will to Live 1:161, 2:162, 3:163, 4:164, 5:166, 6:171, 7:172 (Kap. XIV: Nachträge zur Lehre von der Bejahung und Verneinung des Willens zum Leben).

On the Indestructibility of our Essential Being by Death 1:134, 2:135, 3:136, 4:137, 5:138, 6:139, 7:140, 8:141 (Kap. X: Zur Lehre von der Unzerstörbarkeit unseres wahren Wesens durch den Tod).

On Suicide 1:157, 2:158 (Kap. XIII: Ueber den Selbstmord).

On Women 1:362, 2:363, 3:364, 4:365, 5:366, 6:367, 7:368, 8:369, 9:370 (Kap. XXVII: Ueber die Weiber).

On Thinking for Yourself 1:257, 2:258, 3:259, 4:260, 5:262, 6:263, 7:264, 8:265, 9:267, 10:269, 11:270, 12:271 (Kap. XXII: Selbstdenken).

On Religion: a Dialogue 174 (Kap. XV: Ueber Religion).

On Philosophy and the Intellect 1:1, 2:2, 3:3, 4:4, 5:9, 6:11, 7:12, 8:14, 9:17 (Kap. I: Ueber Philosophie und ihre Methode); 10:22, 11:24 (Kap. II: Zur Logik und Dialektik); 12:31, 13:33, 14:37, 15:38, 16:39, 17:40, 18:41, 19:43, 20:47, 21:48, 22:50,

23:53, 24:54, 25:57, 26:60 (Kap. III: Den Intellekt überhaupt und in jeder Beziehung betreffende Gedanken).

On Ethics 1:109, 2:110, 3:111, 4:113, 5:114, 6:115, 7:116, 8:117, 9:118 (Kap. VIII: Zur Ethik).

On Law and Politics 1:121, 2:122, 3:123, 4:124, 5:125, 6:126, 7:127, 8:128 (Kap. IX: Zur Rechtslehre und Politik).

On Aesthetics 1:205, 2:206, 3:207, 4:208, 5:209, 6:210, 7:212, 8:213, 9:217, 10:218, 11:220, 12:227, 13:228 (Kap. XIX: Zur Metaphysik des Schönen und Aesthetik).

On Psychology 1:305, 2:307, 3:308, 4:310, 5:312, 6:313, 7:315, 8:317, 9:320, 10:321, 11:324, 12:325, 13:326, 14:328, 15:330, 16:331, 17:333, 18:335, 19:336, 20:340, 21:341, 22:342, 23:343, 24:344, 25:346, 26:350, 27:357, 28:358 (Kap. XXVI: Psychologische Bemerkungen).

On Religion 1:175, 2:176, 3:177, 4:178, 5:179, 6:180, 7:181, 8:181A (Kap. XV: Ueber Religion).

On Books and Writing 1:237 (Kap. XX: Ueber Urtheil, Kritik, Beifall und Ruhm); 2:272, 3:273, 4:274, 5:275, 6:281, 7:282, 8:283, 9:284, 10:285, 11:286, 12:287 (Kap. XXIII: Ueber Schriftstellerei und Stil); 13:292, 14:293, 15:294, 16:295, 17:296A, 18:297 (Kap. XXIV: Ueber Lesen und Bücher).

On Various Subjects 1A:71, B:74, C:80, D:94, E:96, F:99 (Kap. VI: Zur Philosophie und Wissenschaft der Natur); 2:69 (Kap. V: Einige Worte über den Pantheismus); 3A:197, B:198, C:199, D:200, E:203, F:203A, G:204 (Kap. XVIII: Einige mythologische Betrachtungen); 4:233 (Kap. XIX: Zur Metaphysik des Schönen und Aesthetik); 5A:238, B:239, C:240, D:242 (Kap. XX: Ueber Urtheil, Kritik, Beifall und Ruhm); 6A:244, B:245, C:248, D:249, E:255 (Kap. XXI: Ueber Gelehrsamkeit und Gelehrte); 7A:372, B:373, C:374, D:375 (Kap. XXVIII: Ueber Erziehung); 8:298 (Kap. XXV: Ueber Sprache und Worte); 9:377 (Kap. XXIX: Zur Physiognomik); 10:378 (Kap. XXX: Ueber Lärm und Geräusch); 11A:385, B:387, C:388, D:399, E:390 (Kap. XXXI: Gleichnisse, Parabeln und Fabeln).